PRA̱ ART
OF ENOUGH

'If you want to have a better life and to make the world a better place then you must read this book. It is wise and practical and beautifully easy to read, everybody should read it.'

Charles Handy, bestselling author of The Empty Raincoat *and* The Second Curve

'Becky has birthed a brilliant and beautifully crafted book. The weave of stories, insights, and exercises are held together by an elegant structure of Seven Arts, making it easy and engaging to follow. If you feel overwhelmed by what's coming at you and want to feel inspired by what's within you, treat yourself to reading and embodying the wisdom of this book.'

Sarah Rozenthuler, Chartered Psychologist, Dialogue Coach and Author of Powered by Purpose *and* How to Have Meaningful Conversations

'A guide to being an even better person, living an even better life and, even in a small way, to making the world a better place, while all the time helping you to ditch the guilt about failing and falling short. Affirmation, Action and Absolution lie within.'

Rev Kate Bottley, Radio 2 broadcaster and Gogglebox vicar

'This is a very empowering, beautifully written book. If you've ever wondered why you end each day feeling overwhelmed, frustrated and just plain worn out, this is the book for you.

The Art of Enough offers sympathetic, pragmatic advice and easy-to-do exercises to help you keep your life (and your mind) in balance.'

'This book not only speaks to me personally, addressing some of the deepest questions about purpose and identity, but it speaks to this present moment in which we all find ourselves – questions about what is most important, our individual place in the world, but also the impact all of this has on the environment. With calm and authoritative wisdom, Becky Hall's profound yet practical book will help us all to reframe our thinking, and know that we are already enough.'

'A wonderfully pragmatic and soulful guide to how we can be more present to our lives, our resources and the world around us for everyone's benefit. A great counterpoint to the excessive individualism and the corresponding exhaustion and depletion our current mindset is producing.'

'At a time when we need more than ever to find balance within ourselves and with the wider world, *The Art of Enough* challenges us to disentangle ourselves, to rewrite our own scripts that allow us to forge greater connection with our environment, those around us, and, importantly, ourselves. A book to be engaged with, not simply read.'

'Becky brings the big, complex questions of our time to our attention in a provocative, yet grounded way. She invites each of us to explore our inner world, so that we may consider how we impact on our outer world too. This book is for those who are curious about how to live with and enable more ease and flow, so that they may be better connected to themselves, those around them, and the beautiful planet we all share.'

Laura Beckingham, seer, coach, writer

'I loved this book. It is beautiful in concept and form and is much needed.'

Lynn Stoney, constellations facilitator and teacher,
Constellations Workshops

'It's often been said that to express something simply, you must first understand it profoundly. *The Art of Enough* is a deceptively simple idea: that if we could learn to find the right balance between scarcity and excess – personally, societally, globally – then we have the chance of a future of flourishing on this planet. But if we really want that, then there is work to do: a lifetime of practising a different way of being, working, loving and living. *The Art of Enough* is a work of compelling coherence: wide-ranging and yet elegantly unified. Drawing from, and speaking to, disciplines including personal development, psychology, physiology, biology, ecology, business management, community development, social theory and spirituality, it is impossible to pigeonhole. In the end, it is a book of wisdom.'

Paul Northup, Creative Director, Greenbelt Festival

'Drawing on a wealth of personal and professional experience, and written with passion and wisdom and insight, Becky Hall offers us another way to live – with a clear guide to the steps we can take to make a change.'

Alison Vickers, coach, facilitator

'It's incredibly honest and grounded yet simultaneously practical and compassionate. I wish I'd read it 25 years ago.'

Judy Parke, secondary school English teacher

'This book is so useful – I keep going back to it. From working-from-home mums, to team leaders and CEOs, discover what matters most and learn the Art of Enough. I would have loved this book while I was feeling overwhelmed as a headteacher, to help me put my life into perspective and achieve a sense of balance.'

Claire White, retired head teacher

'I'm so glad I've read this in my early twenties. It's set me up for finding balance in my life. I found the exercises to build my confidence and make a positive contribution really useful.'

Sarah Wilkinson, educational support worker

'*The Art of Enough* gives us the chance to think and act, from the inside out. Starting with the eco-system of ourselves to the bigger global systems that we know we need to preserve, *The Art of Enough* takes you on a journey, in a timely response to the world's challenges.'

Ruth Overton, organizational development consultant, Investec Bank

7 ways to build a *balanced* life
and a *flourishing* world

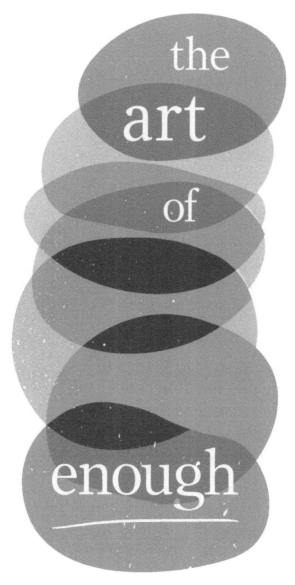

the
art
of
enough

BECKY HALL

First published in Great Britain by Practical Inspiration Publishing, 2021

© Becky Hall, 2021

Illustrations by Daisy Mojave Holland

Back cover photograph by Emma Stokes

ISBN   978-1-78860-289-1   (print)
        978-1-78860-288-4   (epub)
        978-1-78860-287-7   (mobi)

Practical Inspiration
Publishing

MIX
Paper from
responsible sources
FSC® C013604

For Jude, who reminds me daily how to live with the Art of Enough.

I wish you all, every one of you, enough.

Enough sun to keep you bright.

I wish you enough rain so you wish for the sun.

I wish you enough happiness to keep alive your spirit.

I wish you enough pain so the small joys in life seem bigger.

I wish you enough gain to satisfy want.

I wish you enough loss to appreciate what you possess.

I wish you enough 'hellos' to give you strength for the final goodbye.

I wish you enough, so that you wish for nothing more.

Neil Gore, from the play *We Will Be Free!*[1]

CONTENTS

Introduction

WHY WE NEED THE ART OF ENOUGH

Picture the scene. I am sitting opposite Kate,[1] a senior leader who I am coaching. She is telling me that despite her external success and glittering career path, nothing she does can make her feel good enough. No matter how hard she works or how many accolades she receives (which are plentiful), she cannot shake her fear that she is an imposter – waiting to be discovered. This drives her to work relentlessly to achieve a goal that never feels within reach. Kate is stuck in a mindset convinced that she lacks what she needs. She has no permission to rest, and her inner landscape is full of fear. A serial overachiever, she is tired and nothing she does takes her insecurity away. In her mind, she simply cannot *be* Enough.[2]

---

[1] All names used in case studies throughout the book have been changed to ensure anonymity.

[2] A note about grammar. Given that this book is all about finding Enough, it will be written as a proper noun, to create emphasis and clarity; the same applies to the terms Excess and Scarcity.

Now let's zoom in on Omar. Omar is working from home during one of the Covid-19 lockdowns. He has a demanding job and lives in a two-bedroom flat with his wife and their one-year-old son. Omar describes his working life to me; he is at his desk by 7 a.m. and has back-to-back online meetings throughout the day, during which a stream of emails fills his inbox. He takes an hour to be with his wife and son in the early evening, before returning to work late into the evening. He feels overwhelmed by the volume and complexity of what he has to do, and unable to give himself permission to stop either. Understandably, Omar is nearly burnt out with tiredness. It's as if he can never *do* Enough.

And then let's turn our focus to our planet. 'Our house is on fire,' Greta Thunberg said at Davos in 2019.[1] The IPCC report released in October 2018 gives our planet just 12 years to radically alter our carbon usage and emissions to stem catastrophic climate change.[2] Our oceans are now host to plastic islands the size of countries. According to Unicef, across 86% of the UK, children are breathing dangerous levels of toxic air.[3] We are at the start of the 'sixth mass extinction' where thousands of habitats and species are on the verge of extinction driven by ecocide. And yet our response as individuals, societies and institutions is not creating change at sufficient speed. It's as if we don't know how to stop. We can't seem to *have* Enough.

These stories aren't unusual. I've worked to support people and teams for over 20 years; people working hard to give the best of themselves to the businesses, universities, charities, institutions and governments they work for. And what I've noticed is that so many people are out of balance. It's as if we are on a see-saw the whole time, swinging between too much and not enough – oscillating from one extreme to another. Our inner lives are tormented by a lack of inner balance, our outer lives swamped by complexity, while at a meta level the very eco-system of our planet is pushed to breaking point.

I believe that finding the *Art of Enough* from the inside out is the challenge of our age. This book attempts to explore these three fundamental questions.

- Why are we so out of balance in so many areas of our lives?
- How can we find a way of leading our twenty-first-century lives fruitfully, within the limits of Enough?
- What becomes possible for us when we learn to be, do and have Enough?

WHAT IS ENOUGH?

Here's what I mean by Enough. Enough is a state of being and a way of living. With Enough we learn how to live within the natural limits of our lives, and this sets us free to flourish. Enough is resourced by love and abundance. When we believe that we are Enough, we can find freedom and flow that allows us to shine. From a state of being Enough, we can put in place boundaries so that what we do is Enough; we allow ourselves to live and work at a sustainable pace and contribute to making the world a better place for everyone. Enough is a way of living that welcomes the clarity that boundaries can give us and appreciates the renewable power of our resources. Enough gives us the wisdom to follow the natural patterns of growth and transformation that go way beyond always needing more and recognize when we have Enough. Enough connects us to each other and to the planet that we share.

One of the concerns that people have expressed to me about the concept of Enough is that it represents mediocrity – settling for average – not trying hard. I think the reverse is true. Enough allows us each to stand on the fertile ground, well rooted and well resourced so that we can flourish with creativity and brilliance. From our place of Enough, we can grow to be the right size – connecting and contributing to others and our environment so we can do amazing things. We move from the ever-hungry, never-satisfied state of striving to a state of fullness, from which we can thrive. Far from being mediocre, Enough is a springboard to a healthy and sustainable life.

Enough is about returning to a pattern of living which is in tune with that of our planet. Nature's pattern is cyclical. Our ecology for the past ten thousand years has been sustained by a repeating pattern of renewal. It is infinitely abundant. The irony we are now facing, however, is that humankind's exploitation of natural resources over the past few centuries has pushed our ecology away from its pattern of abundant renewal towards a point of scarcity. We have lived with excess, overconsuming natural resources with scant regard for the eco-systems that hold them in balance, to such an extent that we are at a tipping point where we risk running out of the resources needed for life itself. The very *cycle* of renewal is at risk. Seen in this way, Enough is about getting back in sync with the natural rhythms of life, so that we and the planet can flourish again. Whether we are looking at mastering the Art of Enough for our inner lives, our working lives or our collective living, we need to find the balance point between Scarcity and Excess – returning to a pattern of renewal so we can thrive.

James Lovelock's Gaia hypothesis suggests that the world is one living organism held together by interconnected complexity.[4] The famous idea in Gaia is that everything is connected through a series of networked self-organising systems. So, when a butterfly flaps its wings in America, it can set off a chain of mini-changes that can result in a thunderstorm in Africa, which in turn can trigger a hurricane in Asia. In self-organising systems, change starts with small disturbances (like a butterfly flapping its wings), which eventually become amplified by the connected networks within the system to effect big changes elsewhere (like a thunderstorm).

In the same way, I believe that 'Enough' starts with each of us on the inside. For us, small internal changes are the place to start. I have a hunch that there is a deep interconnection between our individual feelings of not *being* Enough, and our experience of being overstretched in our daily lives in service of *doing* Enough, and our inability to stop consuming too much – to say – we *have* Enough. That how we feel on the inside is deeply connected to how much we feel we need to do and ultimately how we can live sustainably together without harming the planet.

This is certainly my lived experience. As a human being making my way, I have had to learn how to find balance in each of these three areas. I've worked hard to feel that I am good enough to be accepted. I've worked hard to manage the huge volume of work that has so often been self-imposed by my desire to prove myself. I've worked hard to balance my deep desire to have a positive impact on the planet with my

5

desire for foreign travel and the convenience of my lifestyle. The irony of all this hard work? I have come to learn that working hard is rarely the answer.

As a coach, I see this so frequently it is hard to ignore the patterns emerging in front of my eyes. So, for both personal and professional reasons, I have gone in search of training, practices, research, stories and guidance that show us how we can find Enough. This is where psychology meets neuroscience, meets systems thinking, meets creative practices. And I have been blessed with many wonderful teachers, therapists, coaches, friends and clients along the way who have helped me in this quest. I hope to share what I have learned with you here.

This book is an invitation to you. What if we, together, explore the Art of Enough as the key to help us get back on track? When I reached out on social media to find others for whom the concept of the 'Art of Enough' resonated, I received so many responses. People have shared their stories, tips and practices with me as they too find their Art of Enough – whether it is how to calm their inner voices, how to manage productivity, workflow and overwhelm, or how they find balance with what they have, what they need and what they consume. In many ways, finding the Art of Enough is a very practical idea. It is also deeply psychological, physiological and even spiritual. The need for balance exists in every aspect of our lives and how we work and live alongside one another. So many of us are working on this stuff – and I think that the more we recognize it, talk about it, celebrate it, the more we can find Enough collectively and appreciate its value.

WHY THE *ART* OF ENOUGH?

Why is finding Enough from the inside out an art? Well, because for each of us it is highly individual. There is not just one way to do this. Our points of balance are different. You will need to create your version of Enough, just as much as I need to find mine. Each of us will have a personal journey to go on to explore how we can feel that we are Enough inside. What I find overwhelming or challenging when balancing my daily life will be different to yours. You have to find your own way – you will know it when you feel it.

Enough is also an art because finding balance can make space for something else to flourish. It's a profoundly creative process. We can't predict what will emerge in us as a result of this state of equilibrium – but liberating ourselves from the tyrannies of too little or too much will create space for something new.

Like any artform, Enough requires intention, creativity, discipline and practice. The Art of Enough is something for you to explore with all your innate resources, your best thinking, your psychology, your creativity, your energy. When you find how to access it, it changes how you live. Throughout this book you will find practices that will help you to be Enough, do Enough and have Enough. An elegant sufficiency. As Goldilocks would say, 'just right!'

THE ART OF ENOUGH MODEL

The Art of Enough is about balance, but what is Enough balancing between? I'm suggesting with the Art of Enough model that rather than being at one end of a binary, Enough is actually poised between two states. Binary thinking is rarely helpful in our complex world – it's more accurate to suggest that we are constantly having to respond to conflicting and complex demands that may tip us off balance. The model offers the state of Enough as the mid-point on a set of scales balanced between the state of Scarcity (too little) on one side and the state of Excess (too much) on the other. Scarcity can be internal: 'I'm not enough,' or external: the fear that there is not enough resource to go around. Similarly, Excess can be individual: 'I am swamped with too much to do,' or collective: overconsuming the world's resources.

The model is deliberately dynamic – Enough is a place of balance that requires constant adjustment. When we find it, it can release a state of creative flourishing, symbolized in our model by a vase of flowers balanced on the top. With Enough, we can blossom and grow.

The Art of Enough model shows how the balance between Scarcity and Excess is built upon seven Arts. Starting from the bottom up, each Art is a guidepost to exploring and finding balance from the inside out. The first three Arts explore the inner challenge of *being* Enough, Arts 4 and 5 look at the outer challenge of *doing* Enough and then Arts 6 and 7 explore the collective challenge of *having* Enough.

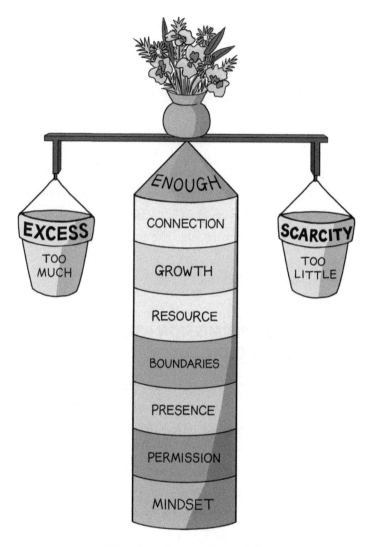

The Art of Enough model
Illustration by Daisy Mojave Holland

Each Art is explored in a chapter of the book. Here's a brief overview of what you can expect.

THE ART OF *BEING* ENOUGH

ART 1: ENOUGH MINDSET – SOURCE YOUR THINKING FROM ABUNDANCE

What is the mindset that underpins your thinking? What are your deepest beliefs, your limiting assumptions about yourself and the world? In Art 1, we explore how what we believe about ourselves and the world shapes how we think. We look at where this might come from and how you can make changes to your mindset. We unpack the mindsets of Excess and Scarcity that can keep us out of balance, and how we can create a mindset of Enough.

ART 2: ENOUGH PERMISSION – THE FREEDOM OF FINDING YOUR BELONGING

Where do your feelings about what you are able to be or do come from? Those voices in your head that hold you back, criticize, judge – whose are they? In Art 2, we explore the hidden dynamics behind who or what you believe you can be. We unpack the unspoken rules of belonging that can keep us trapped in the past and explore how to let go of past entanglements and articulate what is most important to you now – so that you can be Enough on your own terms.

ART 3: ENOUGH PRESENCE – HOW TO MANAGE YOUR STATE TO FIND FLOW

In Art 3, we explore how to find and maintain Enough Presence in our bodies. We look at our neurobiology and learn practices to sustain our state of Enough day in, day out. Art 3 also explores how we can connect our physicality, minds and energy to build our Presence, so that we can take up our space and stand confidently in our own authority, drawing on each moment so that we can embody Enough.

THE ART OF *DOING* ENOUGH

ART 4: ENOUGH BOUNDARIES – THE CLARITY OF COHERENCE

The twenty-first-century digital world is a complex place – full of massive uncertainty and volatility. How can we manage our time, energy and resources so that we do what we can in the time that we have, rather than suffer the crippling anxiety that can accompany overwhelm? Art 4 looks at the benefits of creating healthy boundaries – drawing on the complex adaptive systems in nature and what they do to provide coherence and flow. We explore how to create balance in your work-life that works for your life.

ART 5: ENOUGH RESOURCE – HARNESSING YOUR POWER

In Art 5, we explore the resources we need in order to do Enough. This can mean internal resource – energy, capability, drive – or external resource – time, support, others to delegate to. It is often when we lack resources that we can feel overwhelmed by having too much to do. Art 5 frames Enough Resource as a replenishable cycle, considers ways to avoid burnout and thrive instead, and explores the habits that you can develop in order to sustain a healthy pace of Enough.

THE ART OF *HAVING* ENOUGH

ART 6: ENOUGH GROWTH – THE WISDOM OF GROWING SUSTAINABLY

How can we think about growth in a healthier way, consciously balancing cost and gain? Art 6 challenges the received wisdom that our economies need to grow exponentially and offers a model of Enough Growth that moves beyond our addiction to 'more is better'. We explore contemporary environmental economics and ways of looking at growth that allow us as individuals, businesses and societies to grow in more generative, sustainable ways.

ART 7: ENOUGH CONNECTION – THE LOVE THAT GLUES ENOUGH TOGETHER

Art 7 looks at how we create the 'Art of Enough' together – whether it is with our families, our workplaces, or the communities we live in. We explore the importance of connecting from the inside out – to our own inner sense of being and doing Enough. We explore how important it is to connect with each other and wider still, with our planet – the natural world. When we collectively connect with each other and re-connect with nature, we transform how we behave in relation to it.

PRACTICES FOR EACH ART

Each chapter explores what the Art is about, with case studies and examples woven in to ground the ideas in real-life examples. I have integrated practices within each chapter too, which offer you the chance to reflect on your own life as we go through. I call them practices, because life is rarely about doing something once, and balance certainly isn't. We need to return to things over and over in order to get more comfortable and confident in doing them. Each practice is signposted with a flower or a leaf taken from the vase of flowers symbolising Enough in our model. These are for you to metaphorically collect along the way as you practise finding your state of Enough, making up your own bunch of flowers.

At the end of the book, there is a 'glossary of practices' to remind you of what they all are. Depending on your learning style, you may want to stop and do them at the time or do them at a later date. There are also plenty of reflective questions, intended to give you time and space to think about what Enough means for you in your life and world.

IMAGINAL CELLS: FROM STRIVING TO THRIVING

Throughout the book, I draw on a metaphor of transformation taken from nature – a caterpillar becoming a butterfly. One of the surprising things about metamorphosis is that the cells that will create the transformation from a caterpillar into a butterfly are present within a caterpillar all along. They are poetically called 'imaginal cells'. The caterpillar starts its life unaware of these cells. The first part of its life is simply focused on ravenous consumption. Then the caterpillar forms a chrysalis and dissolves into what's sometimes called an 'organic soup'. This is when the imaginal cells are activated – they hold the vision of the new structure – the butterfly. This is such a powerful metaphor for change: the idea that we carry within us the potential for our own transformation from the outset, often without knowing it.

This image has great resonance in our search for the Art of Enough. Within each of the Arts and perhaps within each of us, there lie imaginal cells: knowledge and potential that we carry, ready to be awakened within us as we find Enough. Journalist Rebecca Solnit draws on this image when she calls for 'the best among us, the most visionary, the most inclusive, to *be the imaginal cells* to get us out of the multiple crises that we face in the early twenty-first century'.[5]

At the end of each chapter, you will see a picture of a butterfly carrying the imaginal cell that I imagine lies at the heart of that particular Art. When we activate our imaginal cells as we learn to be, do and have Enough, perhaps we can move away from the striving that is so much part of the way we live, and start to thrive from the inside out in ways that may – like the butterfly – surprise and delight us.

PART 1

THE ART OF *BEING* ENOUGH

ART 1: ENOUGH MINDSET

SOURCE YOUR THINKING FROM ABUNDANCE

The greatest discovery of my generation is that
human beings can alter their lives by altering their
attitude of mind. If you can change your mind, you
can change your life.[1]

William James

*In Art 1, we will explore the mindset of Enough. For some, not
being Enough can manifest as the well-known phenomenon
of imposter syndrome; for others, it might be a feeling of
inadequacy around not being worthy, or clever or kind –*

the list goes on. We will be looking at how we can move our mindset from one of Scarcity or Excess to Enough – sourcing our thinking from abundance.

We will explore:

- the power of mindset;
- the Scarcity Mindset – the fear of not Enough;
- the Excess Mindset – the fear of too much;
- the Enough Mindset – trust in abundance;
- how to identify your mindset;
- how to re-set.

THE POWER OF MINDSET

John is looking straight at me, through tear-filled eyes.

> The thing is, Becky, I just don't understand how I am doing this job, and I am constantly worried that I'm not up to the task. I feel like a fake the whole time – just pretending to do what I'm doing and waiting until I'm found out. I feel like a kid dressed up in a man's suit, and I'm terrified nearly all of the time.

My client is the CEO of a highly successful legal firm, who has built it up to double the size in the past three years. When I remind him of this fact, he merely responds, 'Well, there was a lot of luck in that. And now the shareholders want me to grow it even more, and I just don't think I'm good enough if I'm honest. I feel like a sham.'

John is far from alone. Have you ever felt that you are not good enough? That it's a fluke that you have your job, and you have to work really hard so people don't find out that you shouldn't really be doing whatever it is you are doing?

I know I have. Sometimes when I'm about to do something – even something that I have done many times before – I can hear a little voice in my head saying, 'How on earth did little old me get to be doing *this*? What do I know?!' This is fine if it's a moment in time – nerves before a big event. 'What if I trip over / forget my lines / say the wrong thing?' It keeps us humble and real and in the moment. What is more concerning for any of us is when this voice presides over everything that we do.

Whenever I mention the Art of Enough, it is the 'not good enough' phrase that first provokes people's interest. I get smiles of recognition – or even responses like – 'OMG yes! I never feel good enough!' It would appear that for many people, across many walks of life, feeling good enough requires work. Imposter syndrome is a real issue for so many of us, and nearly everyone I talk to has experienced a version of it. And of course, it's not only 'good' enough that people recognize. Each of us has our own version of what we lack. For some, it may be not knowing enough, others not being strong enough, or correct enough, or successful enough, or creative enough, or clear enough, or experienced enough, or energetic enough, or acceptable enough. What these all have in common is the inner belief that, somehow, we are lacking what we need to be Enough.

Our underlying inner beliefs shape who we are, what we do and what we allow ourselves to be capable of. In my coaching practice, I see over and over again that what clients hold as core beliefs about themselves and the world, can fundamentally limit or enable who they are and what they do in the world. What you believe becomes crucially defining – if you are living from a belief that you are not Enough then you will constantly be trying to re-balance that by over-compensating in other ways. If you believe that the world is a hostile place or lacks the resources to give you what you need, then it will affect how you interact with it.

It was Carol Dweck who coined the term 'mindset'.[2] Dweck, a psychologist, has spent her career researching the way in which our beliefs about our capability influence how successful we are at achieving our goals and overcoming challenges. For Dweck, 'mindsets frame the running account that's taking place in people's heads. They guide the whole interpretation process.'

Dweck identified two mindsets in particular that define how people approach life: 'growth mindset' and 'fixed mindset'. A fixed mindset is one in which people believe that their skills, intelligence and capabilities are finite – a resource which they have no control over, and which can be compared favourably or unfavourably with others. It is this mindset that leads us to judge ourselves lacking. Dweck's research found that 'the fixed mindset creates an urgency to prove yourself over and over.'

A growth mindset, on the other hand, is one in which we believe that our basic qualities – our skills, capabilities, intelligence – are a starting point from which we can grow. With this mindset, we believe that we can grow and develop, learn from our mistakes and from what we've done well, and allow others to help us. A difficult scenario or setback is thought of as a challenge rather than a limitation. It is not that we are incapable; we simply might require a different approach. Marcel Proust summed this up beautifully when he wrote, 'the real act of discovery consists not in finding new lands, but in seeing with new eyes.'[3] Rather than seeing a setback as insurmountable, we look beyond it to see where a solution could lie.

Here's an example of what this can look like in practice. I was coaching an extremely talented young woman who told me, 'I couldn't possibly apply for that job; I don't have all the experience.' We talked about mindsets and I invited her to apply a growth mindset – the possibility of thinking beyond the problem. She moved from focusing on herself as inadequate to focusing on the purpose of the role and what she could contribute. This led her to, 'I know I adapt quickly and am really good at engaging people, which is, I think, what this role is looking for. Maybe I'll give it a shot.'

If, as Dweck says, mindsets frame our interpretation process, they are an important factor for us to consider in our search for the Art of Enough. How can we re-balance our view that we are not Enough, or that life demands too much? Looking at the Art of Enough model, we see that Enough is finely balanced between Scarcity and Excess. What mindsets lie underneath each of them? And what defines the Enough Mindset that we are looking for? Let's unpack them.

THE SCARCITY MINDSET – THE FEAR OF NOT ENOUGH

The underlying belief of a Scarcity Mindset is that all resources are finite – scarce – and there is a fear that they will run out. It is akin to Dweck's fixed mindset, but goes beyond a belief about our own abilities and draws on a wider belief about the world; that *all* resources will run out and not replenish. Ironically, this can lead us to hoarding and accumulating more, which exacerbates the problem, because when we take too much it creates a negative spiral. Resources become unevenly allocated, the system tips out of balance and our sense of Scarcity is reinforced.

A Scarcity Mindset is fear based and therefore triggers fear responses: fight (for resources); flight (we run away, not able to face the fear that is presenting itself); or freeze (paralysed by a sense of what we lack). When we are coming from this mindset, nothing is ever Enough. Nothing. We cannot possibly be Enough and no one else can be either. The world is to be feared and we have to prepare and protect ourselves – we worry, we hoard and we compare.

Personally, I notice when I am in this mindset when my own judgemental voice becomes loud. I start on myself, and then, because I am feeling in deficit of my own resource, I start on others. When I'm in a Scarcity Mindset, my loudest voice is fearful, judgemental and restrictive – 'I can't,' 'she can't,' 'I shouldn't,' 'they shouldn't,' 'how could we?' Whenever I hear this voice in my head, or this language spoken by others, I ask the question, 'Who does the "should" belong to?'

A Scarcity Mindset is also where imposter syndrome resides. Jessamy Hibberd in *The Imposter Cure*[4] describes imposter syndrome like this: 'if you don't perform to the highest standards, this leads to feelings of shame, anxiety and you wrongly conclude that this reveals something essential about your lack of ability and talent... fear of failure and self-doubt drive the cycle – if you fail, you're sure to be found out.' This cycle of trying but being found wanting by an internal belief that you are not good enough can lead to terrible anxiety and have a profound limit on what you do. Hibberd is herself a clinical psychologist, who specializes in working with people suffering from imposter syndrome. What is significant in her work is that she identifies it as something that has its source in what we believe about ourselves – our mindset.

Scarcity is, of course, not just about imposter syndrome: a Scarcity Mindset can lead us to believe that we don't have Enough of anything. When we start from a deficit position, literally every day can seem full of comparative lack. 'I don't do enough exercise,' 'I didn't get enough sleep,' 'I don't have enough time,' 'I don't have enough talent,' 'I don't have a big enough house/car/salary.' With a Scarcity Mindset, we simply cannot be, do or have Enough of anything. In this place, we compare ourselves with others and we draw on a binary version of the world – they have, so we don't. They are big – so we are small. We are inadequate and there is not Enough to go around. This mindset sees the world's resources as a big cake – once it is eaten, it's gone, and we have to fight for our slice. We are scared that what we have and what others have will run out, or that it was never Enough in the first place.

Another facet of the Scarcity Mindset is a core belief that there is a 'right' way to be. A perfect version of being that we cannot ever live up to. I call this the curse of perfectionism. If we believe there is a perfect way to be, then we will always fall short. Never good enough. This can be devastating to our self-image. Perfection is a fantasy, something that is impossible to attain, and as such, can become a stick to beat ourselves with. Living with a Scarcity Mindset comes at a high cost – it can be exhausting to constantly fear not being Enough. And more than that, it robs us of our joy.

AN EXAMPLE OF THE SCARCITY MINDSET AT PLAY

I have written this book during the coronavirus global pandemic. What I noticed in many of the responses to this huge, existential, life-changing threat is how easy it is for us to get drawn into a Scarcity Mindset. The empty shelves in the supermarkets early in the first lockdown were a testament to that. People were driven by fear and reverted to the very primal instinct to protect themselves. It's all so human – and I'm not immune – none of us are.

When lockdown first happened and everything seemed to be shutting down, I spent hours looking at my business forecast, calculating and re-calculating how long it would be before my business reserves ran out, despite the fact that my work had not in fact dried up. Even though each time I did this, I could reassure myself that I was fine for several months – I just kept going back to doing the same thing. I was stuck in a state of fear. And almost worse than that, I felt unable to connect with others to help me out of this state. It felt shameful and lonely. This was the Scarcity Mindset taking hold, and until I noticed what was going on, I could not begin to make choices to change it.

THE EXCESS MINDSET – THE FEAR OF TOO MUCH

Now, let's look at the other side of the scales: the Excess Mindset. Here everything is too much. There is too much to do, too much to think about, too much to absorb. We have to protect ourselves from the encroaching, ever-hungry, greedy monster who wants to take over our time, our resource, our energy. This is where panic resides, along with anxiety and pressure. Walls fall in and we feel at the mercy of a greater force that can feel impossible to resist. This mindset is also fear based – and our need to protect ourselves leads to pushing back – building walls, moving away.

The threat here is not so much that we'll run out of resource, and more that we will be consumed by the needs of others. This is a boundary issue. We are unable to hold our boundary here: we are swamped. It is quite literally overwhelming, and we can feel powerless and overpowered by too many demands which are beyond our control. I always think of the Wicked Witch of the West from the *Wizard of Oz* as a metaphor for overwhelm. As the fatal bucket of water literally overwhelms her, she dissolves, screeching, 'I'm melting!' In our world that is so complex and uncertain, where digital availability means that we can be contacted at any time, an Excess Mindset can run amok.

While the digital age has brought us massive benefits (perhaps never more so than during the global pandemic), it also presents us with challenges. Our smartphones make us always contactable, which means we can feel the need to be constantly available and responsive. According to research, 53% of us get anxious when we 'lose our mobile phone, run out of battery or credit, or have no network coverage.' There is even a form of clinical anxiety called 'nomophobia', meaning 'no mobile phone phobia'.[5] With an Excess Mindset, we feel perpetually under pressure to respond to a seemingly endless stream of demands on us. We will explore how to address the challenges of this mindset in Arts 4 and 5 later in this book.

AN EXAMPLE OF THE EXCESS MINDSET AT PLAY

One of my former coaching clients, Donal, was a senior operations manager in the transport industry. Donal found it extremely hard to switch off from work in the evenings or weekends and told me that the first thing he did when he woke every morning at 5 a.m. was check his phone. He reported feeling constantly under pressure, and unable to stop. We were working on this – until the session when he told me this story, and everything changed for him.

His beloved father-in-law had died – a man he had loved and respected for over 30 years of his marriage. After the funeral, they went to a golf club for the wake, which he described as being a lovely occasion for a great man. Until he realized that he couldn't find his work phone. He must have dropped it at the crematorium. This sent him into such a panic that he left the wake in full swing to return to the crematorium car park to look for it. As he got there, he saw the red light from his phone blinking at him in the darkness. The momentary relief that he felt was quickly overwhelmed by massive guilt and sorrow. He had left his wife at her father's wake alone, missing the tributes to a man he greatly loved, because he was worried that he would not be contactable for work. This moment of truth changed Donal – and gave huge energy and focus to his intention to re-balance his mindset and find his own Art of Enough.

THE ENOUGH MINDSET – TRUST IN ABUNDANCE

The Enough Mindset that sits in the middle of the scales and moves us away from the fear at either end is rooted in a trust in the abundance of life. It can be tempting, balanced as it is between the strong forces of Scarcity and Excess, to think of it as a place of being simply 'not bad'. However, this is far from the case: it is way more complex and hopeful than that.

First, let's revisit what I mean by Enough. Enough is a place of fullness. Enough is a generative state, full of stretch, growth and ambition to fill our potential – because it moves us beyond our limiting judgements. Enough is a state of elegant balance, where being and doing are finely poised in equilibrium, deeply interconnected. An Enough Mindset offers us a way of being and believing that is sourced by love and abundance. There is Enough. We can do Enough. We are Enough.

In the course of my own learning journey and field research working with hundreds of coaching clients, I've identified three elements that make up an Enough Mindset.

ENOUGH MINDSET #1: ENOUGH COMES FROM LOVE, NOT FEAR

An Enough Mindset is based on a belief that we are loveable exactly as we are – with all our flaws and talents. Of course, we can change and grow, but as a starting point, we are simply who we are and that is Enough, in and of itself. Tara Brach calls this 'radical self-acceptance'.[6] For many of us, this is the work: to spend time learning to accept ourselves, and to go further than that – to love ourselves. My father once told me that the antidote to fear is love. This chimes with me because when I'm feeling fearful, I notice that I'm immediately more critical of myself and others. When we switch to the Enough Mindset, we can re-set our fear to love; where we are loveable and most importantly we treat ourselves with love. This can turn our fear of not being Enough on its head, because when we love something or someone, we are kind to them – we want them to learn, to grow, to do well.

From an Enough Mindset, our shortcomings are not permanent: they are learning points. The mistakes we make aren't because we always make them but because we did this one time. If we didn't do our best at something, it's not because we are personally incapable, but because we weren't feeling great that day. If we do something less than brilliantly, it doesn't mean we are hopeless – simply that we are trying – and sometimes that's good Enough. And when it's not, we can work to do it better, safe in the knowledge that it can never be perfect because the human condition isn't perfect.

 PRACTICE 1: APPRECIATION

One thing that can really help here is to learn to notice the things that you appreciate about yourself. The positive impact of this practice is well documented and can help move you from a position of Scarcity to one of abundance. Focusing on what you value in yourself and in your life, however small, moves you into appreciating what you *are*, rather than what you lack.

- Start keeping a note each day of three things that you appreciate about yourself.
- It may help to include here things that you are grateful to yourself for having done. Recognising your own efforts is a great way to combat the perfectionist gremlin.
- This can then extend out to interactions you have with others, or simply things you are grateful for within your life. By recognising how good things are, we awaken a sense of gratitude.

Practising appreciation regularly helps us access joy every day in small moments, which in turn keeps us firmly in an Enough Mindset. When we are able see ourselves as complete, full, Enough, we can face whatever life throws at us. As Maya Angelou puts it: 'You alone are enough – you have nothing to prove to anybody.'

ENOUGH MINDSET #2: ACKNOWLEDGE THINGS AS THEY ARE AND FOCUS ON WHAT'S THERE IN THE MOMENT

An Enough Mindset starts from a position of seeing the world as it is, not as it should be. In *The Book of Joy*,[7] His Holiness the Dalai Lama and Archbishop Desmond Tutu teach us that any change needs to start from an acknowledgement of how things are. They say, 'We cannot succeed by denying what exists. The acceptance of reality is the only place from which change can begin.'

Acknowledging things as they are means that we have to start from the present moment, not an idealized view of what should be. With an Enough Mindset, we can see that perfection is a fantasy, so we release ourselves from its clutches. Sure, we can aim for excellence – but we do this from a position of knowing that giving the best of ourselves to things that matter to us will be Enough. We seek flow in what we do rather than constantly pushing ourselves to work more or harder.

The psychoanalyst and writer Donald Winnicott famously coined the term 'good enough mother' to describe what his research revealed to be the healthy response of a mother to her child.[8] He observed that the primary need of a mother is to be responsive to the needs of her baby in the moment. When I became a parent, I thought to myself, 'I don't want to just be good enough, I want to be amazing!' I hadn't understood the deeper requirements of what Winnicott is describing here. To meet the needs of a baby, to be 'good enough' on their terms, requires something that takes real skill and commitment to achieve. A level of attentiveness to the present moment, an acknowledgement that all babies are different and have their own specific needs, and a mother's ability to empathize with and focus on the needs of her child more than her own thoughts and feelings about what she 'should' be doing. Winnicott teaches us that when a mother gives neither too little, nor too much, but just Enough to fulfil each baby's individual needs, the child will develop in a psychologically healthy way. This moves us beyond the binary concepts of success and failure, and towards something much more inclusive and wise: that to be Enough is the starting point for thriving.

ENOUGH MINDSET #3: THE WORLD IS ABUNDANT – RESOURCES ARE REPLENISHABLE

An Enough Mindset sees the pattern of life as one of abundant renewal. Because we are in a state of balance, resources that have become depleted renew when we give them space to do so. We take our blueprint from the cyclical pattern of nature, where replenishment is as inevitable as the turning of the year; the re-growth of spring always follows the hibernation of winter. So it is for us: we too live in cycles; we get hungry – we need to eat. We get tired, so we can rest.

When we tune in to this pattern and learn to trust it, we can find that the fear of Scarcity and of Excess can be replaced by a trust in love and abundance. What we have, what we offer and what we consume is plentiful, renewable and sufficient for what we require. When we believe this, we can relax in the knowledge that there is Enough resource to give us what we need.

HOW TO IDENTIFY YOUR MINDSET

Having explored the three mindsets of Scarcity, Excess and Enough which can do so much to help or hinder the Art of Enough, let's explore how you can identify what your mindset is, and what you can do to change it. Many of us go through our lives on autopilot without noticing our mindset, let alone challenging what our underlying beliefs are. Partly because they feel so much part of us. We're like a goldfish swimming around in the bowl: a passer-by asks, 'How's the water?' to which the goldfish replies, 'What's water?' How do we know what our beliefs are when we are so familiar with them that we don't even realize that another way is possible?

What we believe to be true about ourselves and our interaction with the world is formed from a very young age and is influenced by a complex mix of nature and nurture. Our perception of what's possible for us can change with our own experiences too, of course. We might fear we can't do something, then when we achieve it, we realize we can after all. But it doesn't always impact on our deepest beliefs. Until we bring these out into the open, it's hard to challenge them or to offer ourselves a choice about our view of the world.

The key is to start to notice your own patterns so that you can bring them to light and give yourself some choices. To do this, it can help to focus on three things:

1. What you are telling yourself
2. The language that you are using
3. Your emotions

1. WHAT YOU ARE TELLING YOURSELF

Inner beliefs can be buried deep, and our brains like familiarity and work in patterns. The key to identifying them is to really start to listen in and notice the voices in your head. Imagine that your thoughts really are separate voices. The Pixar film *Inside Out* wonderfully brings this to life by personifying each human emotion as a character. Sometimes it can simply be a question of speaking your thoughts out loud or writing them down. Bringing your thoughts to life in this way allows you to notice what you are telling yourself you can and can't do.

Here are some examples from my own playbook:

'If you speak up now, you'll look like an idiot.'
'Everyone here knows so much more than you.'
'You don't know what you're doing here.'
'You could never do that – you're not clever enough.'

Once you have noticed the voices, you can start to identify your own patterns and the assumptions you are making. In my case, using the voices above, I could quite quickly see that these voices were all fear based: all Scarcity Mindset. The next step is to ask the question, 'What am I assuming here?' By deliberately using a verb we place the emphasis on what we are able to change so we can focus on that. Lots of the assumptions we make don't really belong to us – they are loyalty to someone or something else (we'll explore this in Art 2).

Coach Nancy Kline in *Time to Think*[9] calls these limiting assumptions, which hold us back and 'make it impossible for the thinker's ideas to flow further'. Kline offers a great way of turning what these 'limiting assumptions' are on their head once you have identified them. It comes in the form of what she calls an 'incisive question'. I've outlined the process in the practice below, adding in the element of Enough.

 PRACTICE 2: ASKING INCISIVE QUESTIONS

- Identify the limiting assumption being made. This can be done on your own by writing down what you say to yourself as I did above, or by someone (a coach, colleague, friend, or what Kline calls a 'thinking partner') really listening to you verbalising your thoughts and repeating them back to you, so that you can identify the assumptions behind the words.

- You (or your thinking partner) then asks, 'What is my limiting assumption?'

- Let's say the limiting assumption from my playbook is 'I am not clever enough to speak out.'

- 'Do you think it's true that you're not clever enough to speak out?'

- You might respond: 'No… not *really*'. Therefore, you know you have uncovered a limiting assumption. Something that you carry as an inner belief that is not actually true.

- Once you've identified the limiting assumption, it is time to think of an alternative using an Enough Mindset and put words to that. We're not looking for the opposite here – that would be unhelpfully binary. What you are looking for is a counterpoint belief that could offer you a different way of seeing things. Your thinking partner might ask you, 'What would be truer to say? What might be a liberating alternative? What would be Enough?'

- You might respond, 'Actually, I think I am curious and enthusiastic.'
- Then create your incisive question – which goes like this: 'If you knew that you are (insert Enough belief) what would become possible for you?'

So, in our example: 'If you knew that you were curious and enthusiastic, what would become possible for you?'

- Ask yourself the incisive question. Speak or write down your answers. Keep asking the question until you run out of things to write or say. It's amazing how different the answers can be.
- Select one of your answers and practise repeating it. It will help to form a new assumption in line with your Enough Mindset.

2. MIND YOUR LANGUAGE

The second clue in working out what your mindset is at any given time is to notice not only what you say, but how you say it. The father of positive psychology, Martin Seligman, describes in *Learned Optimism*[10], the impact of pessimism on our patterns of self-talk. His research found that there is a strong pull towards what he called the 3 Ps. They are:

- Personalization – that whatever is happening is somehow your fault. 'Why am I so stupid?'

- Pervasiveness – that because something is going wrong in one area of your life, it must be going wrong in all areas of your life. 'I can't get anything right.'
- Permanence – that the challenges you are facing at the moment will never end. 'I'm never going to be able to learn this'.

You'll see that the examples I have given you are full of tell-tale language for each of the 3 Ps. When you start hearing yourself using self-blaming words, judgemental words, permanent words, you can guess that you are coming from a mindset of Scarcity or Excess.

 PRACTICE 3: PATTERNS OF SELF-TALK

1. Start by noticing the voices in your head.
   - When you hear a critical voice, write down what it is saying.
   - What language is your critical voice using?
   - Are you defaulting to 3 Ps' assumptions?
   - What's the tone of voice?
   - What is the mindset behind your voice?
2. Now invite a new voice using an Enough Mindset.
   - What would this voice say to you?
   - What language and tone of voice is used this time?
   - Write it down next to the first voice.
3. Try practising replacing your critical voice with an Enough voice.

4. Notice the impact of using this alternative voice – write it down next to the first two sentences.

3. NOTICE YOUR EMOTIONS

Another key to identifying what mindset you are using is to notice your emotions. What are you feeling at any given moment in response to the challenges you face? If you notice that you feel fear, for example, that will help you identify a Scarcity Mindset. If it is overwhelm, it may be an Excess Mindset. This takes practice.

 PRACTICE 4: OBSERVING EMOTIONS

Try getting really specific when observing your emotions.

- What exactly are you feeling?
- Where is the feeling located in your body?
- What's happening physiologically?

We'll explore the impact of feelings on your physiology in detail in Art 3. But for now, this practice can help get you into the habit of noticing what you're thinking and feeling, so that you can identify the mindset that underpins your experience of the world.

LEARNING TO RETURN TO THE ENOUGH MINDSET

The Enough Mindset is a place of balance and, as we know, balance is dynamic and requires constant adjustments. We may need to re-balance several times a day, especially when we are breaking old habits of thinking and deep-seated belief systems. The good news is that it is entirely possible for us to change our mindset. What I have learned over years of research and working with clients is that the key to changing our patterns is summed up in this process:

1. Notice
2. Pause to reflect
3. Choose
4. Re-set

The first step in returning to your own version of an Enough Mindset is to notice your patterns with the curiosity of a detective. What clues can you glean from yourself about your assumptions about yourself and the world? What do you notice about how you are feeling? What does that tell you about the mindset you are adopting – where you are coming from? This is careful, conscious work. It is a moment-by-moment approach requiring you to notice, notice, notice. Once you have mastered the art of noticing what your mindset is, you can pause to reflect, offer yourself a choice, and consciously change where you are coming from. You are in control of what you believe is possible. When you choose the Enough Mindset, you are choosing to believe in yourself and the abundance of the world. You are choosing to believe that you *are* Enough.

SUMMARY OF *ENOUGH MINDSET*

- Our mindset underpins what we believe about ourselves and the world.

- Scarcity and Excess Mindsets are both driven by fear.
- The antidote to fear is love.
- Imposter syndrome comes from using a Scarcity Mindset.
- The Enough Mindset is built on self-acceptance, love and abundance.
- You can identify your mindset by noticing your assumptions, your language and your emotions.
- You can change your mindset by offering yourself alternative options.
- The sequence for changing your mindset is notice, pause to reflect, choose and re-set.

The transformative potential within an Enough Mindset is...

...cultivating abundance

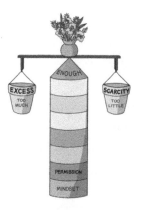

ART 2: ENOUGH PERMISSION

THE FREEDOM OF FINDING YOUR BELONGING

No-one can make you feel inferior without
your consent.

Eleanor Roosevelt[1]

In Art 2, we are going to focus how it feels to give ourselves permission to be Enough – and what makes us feel that we do not have that permission. We will look at how we can let go of versions of our self that don't belong to us: attitudes and opinions that we carry from our past, which hold us back from believing that we are Enough in the here and now. We will explore how we can find a sense of belonging that gives us the freedom to be Enough so that we can flourish in our own ways.

We will explore:

- *why Enough Permission matters;*
- *what do you expect?*
- *rules of belonging;*
- *whose beliefs are you carrying?*
- *let go to let come;*
- *your identity, purpose and values;*
- *the freedom of your own permission.*

WHY ENOUGH PERMISSION MATTERS

Michelle Obama writes in her autobiography *Becoming*[2] about her journey of defying the expectations of what was possible for her as a working-class, young black woman from the poor side of town. She always had the belief of her family, but the sense of low expectations of her from others required her to source her belief from within. She went from internalising the often racist beliefs of others that she was not good enough, to giving herself permission to forge her own beliefs about her potential, so that she was later able to say, having graduated from an Ivy League university and started a first-rate job, 'Am I enough? Yes I am.' Elsewhere, she says, 'I have learned that as long as I hold fast to my beliefs and values, and follow my own moral compass, then the only expectations I need to live up to are my own.'[3] She learned to give herself permission to thrive.

In my first career as an actor, I played Hamlet in an all-female production, touring internationally. It was always interesting saying the most famous lines: they are so well known that the challenge was to make them sound like fresh thoughts. 'To be or not to be, that is the question' was one of those lines of course. Despite having said it hundreds of times, each time I spoke the words I was struck by how much they resonated. I have come to think of this sentence in the context of permission – permission to be exactly who you are. Permission to be or not to be Enough.

I use the term permission because so often we find it hard to find our balance because we perceive that we are not allowed to *be* balanced. Enough Permission is all about exploring the deep-rooted feelings and entanglements that keep us trapped in a state of Scarcity or Excess, even when we have identified and worked on our Enough Mindset. Because, as we all know, thinking about something is not all there is – we have to feel it too. Dr Lauri Santos, director of Yale University's Science of Happiness programme, calls this the 'GI Joe Paradox'.[4] Even though we know something to be true, it doesn't change anything until we inhabit it, or act on it. Knowledge is only part of the picture. My coaching friend Michael Cahill puts it like this: 'You can't *think* your way out of something you've *felt* your way into.' The array of feelings within Scarcity and Excess are strong – and until we identify and articulate them, they attach themselves to our beliefs and retain a strong, compulsive hold over us.

It is the assumptions and beliefs that we hold about ourselves and the world that often keep us entangled in a state of Scarcity. We are comforted by their familiarity and the sense of belonging they can give us. They may not even be beliefs that we hold anymore, but they are so entrenched and embodied into our habits of thinking and being that

41

it takes some work to disentangle them. Giving ourselves permission to be Enough, to say no to this past Scarcity and yes to future abundance, requires us to look a little bit more deeply into our beliefs and assumptions – this time, not only with our heads but with our hearts.

Let me give you a personal example of this. It was in the late 1980s that I realized that I was gay. At that time, pretty much everything around me told me that this was at worst sinful, and at best problematic. When I came out, I was told by people close to me that I had 'chosen' a difficult path and one that would considerably limit my career, prospect of having a family and my life chances. Society at that time told me the same, and it was legally true too. AIDS was at its peak – the 'gay disease' killing thousands of gay men – and Section 28 was still enshrined in law meaning that it was illegal in the UK to 'promote homosexual lifestyles' or even suggest that being gay was acceptable, let alone a completely valid way to live an authentic life. So, I learned to adjust who I came out to in a work context (less so in my personal life – I have loving friends and family to thank for that). That was over 30 years ago of course, and how times have changed! Our two teenage daughters, who we worried might get bullied for having three gay parents (my wife and I co-parent with our best friend Johnty), have never batted an eyelid about their heritage – apart from sometimes complaining it takes a long time to explain! Over the years of course, I have done a lot of work on self-acceptance and learning to re-frame the deeply homophobic beliefs that I carried inside myself from my upbringing, in order to learn that I really can be who I am. And yet... still now, after all this time, I can find myself hesitating – usually in a work setting – if someone asks me, for example, what my 'husband' does. In those moments, I can find a bolt of tension running through my body – full of shame, loneliness and the fear of not belonging. Cognitively, I have re-set my belief system and mindset, but inside I still have to engage in practices that remind me, each day, that who I am is acceptable. That I too can belong. In those moments, I need to draw heavily on my self-written permission to be who I am. Enough.

Choosing to break the bonds of former belief systems can give us agency, which in turn helps us to tolerate the discomfort of having to re-frame our view of ourselves and the world. This is why permission is so important. What I'm recommending here is so much more than simply having permission to be who we are and be accepted as such. Enough Permission is about having the freedom to grow, to develop, to be our best selves, to flourish. To burst out of the limits that we or others may have put on ourselves and to give ourselves permission to shine brightly from the platform of knowing that we are Enough.

Centuries ago, St Augustine wrote: 'People go abroad to wonder at the heights of mountains, at the huge waves of the sea, at the long courses of the rivers, at the vast compass of the ocean, at the circular motions of the stars, and they pass by themselves without wondering.'[5] I love this quote because it reminds us that, while looking outwards can be wonderful, it is looking inwards where we can find the 'vast compass' of our own depths, the 'circular motions' of our joy, wonder at our true selves – and in doing so find our freedom. It's a journey to inner space. Once we do this, we give ourselves a sense – a felt sense – of what it is like to have permission to say yes to flow and abundance.

WHAT DO YOU EXPECT?

Let's start with unpacking our expectations of ourselves and where these come from. What is it that you believe yourself capable of – or not? What expectations, hopes if you like, do you have about what you can achieve? Many people I work with are crystal clear about what they are aiming to do with their lives – in relation to their career paths or life events. And many people I work with haven't given it a second thought, focusing on what is there in front of them, and taking each opportunity as it comes. In some ways, it doesn't matter which camp you fall into: we are all different and find our paths in different ways – and we may move between camps at different points in our life. However, it is in the moments when we are somehow not progressing – when there seem to be immovable roadblocks (inner or outer) to what we are trying to achieve – that we meet the need to explore our deeper beliefs. Where do they come from, who do they really belong to, and are they are still serving us? What are the hidden dynamics at play that may be stopping you from achieving your deepest desires?

I have spent a lot of my adult life developing practices that give less power to what others think of me, and on drawing my sense of being Enough from my own inner compass. For some of us, it's a challenge to believe we are Enough from the inside – not looking to other people, jobs, status, recognition to do this for us. Again, these expectations are often a product of our earlier life experiences, which, until we are conscious of them, can keep us entangled. For example, I grew up as the third child in a sibling group of four, where academic success was highly valued. My elder sister and brother were both very successful academically and I lived in the shadow of this, finding my own way to get attention (usually noisily!). This left me with a legacy of having to prove myself as 'clever' and driving myself to be successful in exhausting ways. Pushing to prove myself as worthy of attention and love is for me a historic pattern that I wasn't conscious of until I started to explore why I was striving so hard. I was the one driving myself to over-achieve and 'be successful' in response to something that was no longer relevant and certainly not serving me, but nonetheless deeply felt. I realized that the permission to be Enough had to come from me.

Life coach Gay Hendricks, in *The Big Leap*,[6] talks about a phenomenon he's noticed which he calls 'the upper limit problem'. He describes a pattern whereby people who are poised to move on to a new level of success or accomplishment inexplicably self-sabotage their own prospects. Their lack of inner belief in their potential simply won't let them achieve what they are capable of. I've observed this in my practice too, in terms of career development and also in other ways. Our beliefs cover much more than our careers: they can limit our ability to do all sorts of things – from finding and maintaining relationships to succeeding in a sports challenge we might set ourselves. It takes enormous insight and courage to be disloyal to beliefs that we have held for a lifetime.

RULES OF BELONGING

Let's explore what it is that might be holding us back in those moments. When I posed the question about what your expectations of yourself were, who else did you think of? Was it just you, or was there someone else in your mind's eye? So often when we think about what we want to achieve, we find that there is another influence in our minds. It could be a parent, a sibling, a teacher. Someone who has had a big influence over us (positive or negative) from an early start in our lives.

'The deepest human need is to belong,' says John Whittington in his book, *Systemic Coaching and Constellations*,[7] and he continues, 'belonging can only occur with others, in a system, a relationship system.' Think about the first system that you were a part of – your family of origin. What were the rules of belonging, spoken or unspoken? What was smiled on, approved of by your family when you were growing up, and what was frowned on or outright forbidden? Many of our deepest beliefs, whether we like them or not, come from this early influence and we can carry them, unchecked and unchallenged, throughout our lives. In psychology, this is called the 'imprint phase'. Ninety percent of our values and beliefs are formed by the age of ten years old. Of course, many of these can be immensely resourcing and give us profound strength. And some of them can be equally unhelpful. The two key beliefs that limit and enable us are those we hold about ourselves and those we hold about what the world is like.

 PRACTICE 5: RULES OF BELONGING

Here's a really practical way of bringing this to life for you.

- Thinking about your family of origin, draw a square on a piece of paper.
- Inside the square write down the 'rules of belonging': the beliefs that were present in your family, even if

they were implied and not stated. This can be things like, 'We work hard,' 'We don't like to take life too seriously,' 'It's good to keep quiet about feelings,' or 'If we disagree, we tell each other – better to argue than stew.' These rules can extend beyond behaviours to expectations about what your family believed possible for belonging, such as, 'Only the sons of the family work in the family business,' 'We don't go to university in our family' – or even something more explicitly labelled such as 'We're an army family' or 'We're a Christian family'.

- Now think about the rules – stated or implied, that signal *not* belonging. Again, this can be behaviours, 'making a scene', 'showing off', 'not working hard', or it can be things that people do: 'mothers who go out to work full time', 'people with no faith', 'people who smoke'. Write these down on the outside of the square on your paper.

- Look at the rules – both inside and outside the square. Underline the ones that still have any power over you, which you still consciously or even secretly believe to be true.

- It can be useful to repeat this exercise with other significant systems you have been part of: your schools, your faith community, your friendship groups, organizations you've worked in. What were the rules of belonging there?

This exercise can start to help you unpack and notice the rules of belonging that you have picked up throughout your life and continue to live by. Some of them will continue to resource you and give you a positive sense of identity. Others may have been very useful at some point in your life but may not serve you any longer. You may very well have already consciously broken the rules. This means that you will have been disloyal to the rules of your family. For example, people who are the first in their families to go to university, or children who are more successful as adults in their careers than their parents. While the family may be really proud, often the person who leaves to go and study feels a sense of disconnect – of disloyalty to the family they come from. This can then lead to a great sense of isolation and loneliness – a feeling of not belonging. It is this idea of loyalty or disloyalty to a system that you have been a part of that is so useful to become aware of.

To add a layer of understanding of how this can influence our experience, Bert Hellinger (the founding father of this systemic approach) teaches us that every system has what is called a 'conscience group' – a moral code that underpins the rules of belonging within it. This conscience group will profoundly impact what we believe to be acceptable (which allows us to feel innocent) or unacceptable (which makes us feel guilty) within the group we are part of. If something we want to do in life breaks the rules of our family system's conscience group, then we feel guilty. If we stay within our family's conscience group, we feel innocent. Hellinger said, 'there is no growth without guilt'.[8] He meant that we sometimes have to break the rules of belonging within conscience groups or systems from our past, in order to thrive and grow in the present. When we do this, it can make us feel guilty because we are being disloyal to something we once belonged to.

One of my teachers in this work, Lynn Stoney, explains the strong hold a conscience group has, using the example of a terrorist.[9] If someone commits an atrocity – for example, plants a bomb that kills people – that is in keeping with the beliefs of their conscience group, then they can remain innocent in their own eyes. The atrocity that they commit is permissible for them because the cause is loyal to the beliefs held within their conscience group. There will, of course, be other layers and factors at play in such an extreme example, but it demonstrates how people can do really serious things 'in good conscience' when it binds them to their group and makes them innocent in their eyes. As GK Chesterton once wrote, 'The soldier fights not because he hates what is in front of him, but because he loves what's behind him.'[10] Guilt and innocence in this context are more to do with belonging and loyalty to a conscience group than to do with an overarching moral code. I use this example because it demonstrates how deeply held these beliefs are and how much they give us permission (or not) to act in the world.

Let's bring it back to you. Hellinger suggests that the movement from one system to another requires a transfer of loyalty. When you inhabit a familiar system, you know and understand the hidden rules of belonging and whether you ever articulate them or not, you comply with them. You remain innocent. When you are trying to change your frame, or enter a new system, it means that you necessarily become 'guilty' to the first system you are leaving. It is these hidden loyalties that can stop us from making the long-term change – unless we know what they are, we remain 'blindly loyal' to the first system.

In order to move from one system to another, we may well feel disloyal – guilty even – and guilt is not a comfortable feeling. It's one thing to understand that we want to change but feeling our way into it is very different. Our ability to change can be restricted by our ability to tolerate discomfort, guilt and sometimes even a profound sense of isolation and loneliness. It is sometimes easier and more comfortable to stick to our old loyalties – a familiar sense of belonging. However, although transition is not always easy and can feel deeply uncomfortable at first, it is like putting on new leather shoes that need to be worn in. Once we've worn them a few times and they have moulded to our feet, we can settle into our new way of being. We belong again, but this time having made choices that serve us better for where we are now.

WHOSE BELIEFS ARE YOU CARRYING?

Let me give you an example of how this can play out. Frances is a talented executive director of a large organization. In her late thirties, she often found herself feeling overlooked in meetings with her peers and CEO on the executive team she was part of. She contacted me for coaching, asking initially for work on her presence, her voice, her body language, so that she could be heard and listened to when she spoke up. When I asked the reason that she wanted to start there, she explained that she wanted to work on building her authority and gravitas, so that she could be 'taken more seriously as a director, especially by my mostly older, male colleagues'.

As we began the work, I wondered if there was something in her past systems that she was still being loyal to, which was holding her back from feeling comfortable with her own authority. I started by asking her about what might give her strength from her family system.

> 'Who would smile to see that you have made it to be a director of a large institution?'

> 'Oh, that'll be my gran – my dad's mum,' she said, as quick as a flash, 'she always believed in me.'

We put a marker down on the floor to represent her gran, who resourced and believed in her.

> 'And who are you being loyal to when you are not being heard or listened to.'

Again, without a beat:

> 'My mum. She was always telling me to be quiet, to go to my room, to get out from under her feet. She didn't want me to make a fuss. She never worked and I felt like she never believed that I would either. I was the first to go to uni in my family, so I left home when I was 18 and have been independent since. I still think she feels like I have no right to be successful. I can almost feel her incredulity.'

We put a marker down on the floor to represent her mother.

> 'And which of these women do you believe to be right?'

> 'Both of them. I sometimes feel really big and responsible, and other times I feel like a little girl without a voice. It's like there are two versions of me.'

As we unpacked her experiences, Frances realized that part of her was being loyal to her mother's beliefs about the world, which were that women didn't work or have the right to a voice in the world. This mirrored her mother's personal experience of life. Her gran, on the other hand (her father's mother), didn't have that view, and always thought that Frances would 'go far'.

As we worked on her family system, Frances was able to thank her gran for her belief and faith in her – acknowledging it as a continuing resource in her life, even though her gran was no longer alive. Frances also realized that she was carrying a belief about her right as a woman to have a voice that didn't belong to her – it was her mother's, and it was holding her back. Together, we created some words for Frances to say to the representative of her mother so that she could respectfully return this belief with her.

> Mum, I know that I have had opportunities in my work and life that you never had. The belief that women shouldn't work rests with you and your experience. The part of it that is mine I'll keep, and the part of it that is yours, with the greatest of respect, I leave with you. Please smile on me as I learn how to inhabit my authority as a senior leader in my organization.

This simple act of acknowledging, returning responsibility and asking for blessing to walk a different path had a profound effect.

Bert Hellinger describes this work of looking back systemically as 'restoring the flow of life and love' by 'joining things that have been wrongfully separated, and separating things that have been wrongfully joined'. In this case, Frances had been carrying her mother's belief unintentionally and unconsciously, and it had been holding her back from inhabiting her own authority and really believing that she had permission to be in the role she was in. She needed to break the rules of belonging that she had grown up with and create new ones so that she could grow into her new system of inner belonging. We never needed to do any voice work. Frances's gravitas began to expand once she had released herself from the hidden belief that she had no right to it.

 PRACTICE 6: HIDDEN LOYALTIES

Try applying this to you. What are the beliefs you hold about what you can and can't do? Write them down. Now reflect on these questions:

- Who would smile on you as you act on that belief?
- Who are you being loyal to in maintaining that belief?
- Is that belief still serving you now, or holding you back?
- Is it yours or does it belong to someone else?
- What beliefs do you want to let go of so that you can grow?

As in the example of Frances, when I ask these questions in coaching, people often know immediately where the source of their limiting beliefs comes from. It emerges from them almost like an instinct – a felt sense – something that they have literally embodied and carried as theirs for a long time. You might find that too. If you realize that you are being loyal to a belief that doesn't belong to you, but someone in your past, or that you no longer want to carry a belief that is not serving you, you can very respectfully find a way to return it to who it does belong to. You don't have to carry it anymore. You can keep the bit of it that does belong to you or continues to serve you and return the belief to its rightful place. Then you are free to turn to your future resourced by the systems you have belonged to, not constrained by them.

This is deep work for the Art of Enough. It is often the beliefs that we carry about what we lack, or about what we need to do in order to find love or approval, that push us consciously or unconsciously into sourcing our feelings from Scarcity or Excess. For us to free ourselves to live with ease and self-sufficiency balancing the Art of Enough, we sometimes need to look back and untangle the beliefs that underpin so much, but that are no longer true for us. And we need to give ourselves permission to be Enough in the present, so that we can continue to learn and grow.

LET GO TO LET COME

One of my favourite phrases is, 'let go to let come'. If we are able to identify and let go of things we are carrying that no longer serve us – beliefs, limiting assumptions, old entanglements – then we can put ourselves into the state to let whatever is next emerge. In *Theory U: Leading from the Future as it Emerges*,[11] Otto Scharmer describes this process as 'presencing'. Allowing your 'open mind, your open heart and your open will' to open the possibility for something else. From this state, we can begin to let the future emerge. So far in Art 2, we have focused on the letting go part of this process. Moving away from a state of Scarcity at one end of our scales or the feeling of Excess at the other and into the state of Enough where with an open mind, heart and will, we can start to re-create what is possible.

Now is the time to decide what you *do* have permission for. Think of it as creating your new springboard. Owning what you are capable of, learning to believe it. This transition is like having two radios – an old one and a new one. Over time, you will be able to turn down the volume of the old radio and turn up the volume of the new one, until eventually, it is all you can hear. In this way, you will create the neural pathways you require to be who you are now – something that we will explore in more detail in Art 3. For this transition stage, I like to think in terms of 'permission slips'. You know, like the ones that your parents had to sign when you were a kid to say you can go on a school trip. What is your new intention that you are teaching yourself is ok? What are the new rules of belonging for the new system you are moving into?

 PRACTICE 7: PERMISSION SLIPS

Returning to the exercise you did earlier in this chapter, draw a square in the middle of a piece of paper.

- What are the rules of belonging for you in your life now? Intentional rules, which give you permission to be and do what feels Enough for you. If it's useful, write these down as your 'permission slips'.
- What are the things – the rules – that you absolutely want to leave out of the square? You may want to say

goodbye to them, thank them even, for having served you in the past but no longer having a use for you in the present.

Setting your own intentions about what you can and can't do, what you want to be able to achieve and how you want to be, can feel, in the context of inner beliefs, a little far-fetched. But you may be pleasantly surprised. The more you are able to articulate and make conscious the things that you want to achieve, the more accessible to you they will become. You have control over this, because it is your life you are talking about. This is self-actualization in its deepest form: you are actualising what your soul wants to become and not what your ego craves.

YOUR IDENTITY, PURPOSE AND VALUES

One way of finding an articulation of your Enough Permission – who you want to be in the world – is to get really clear about your identity, your core purpose and your values. It can be useful to think of these three things as a hierarchy. We know who we are (our identity) when we know what we are here to do (our core purpose) and the reason for doing it (our values). Distinguishing each of these can provide us with real clarity. When they become tangled, it can hold us back. For example, if our values become our identity, then who we are becomes confused with what we believe – and this can become profoundly limiting. People whose entire identity is built around their political beliefs, for instance, risk never feeling able to change their views or grow in new or different ways. Let's explore how we can articulate our core purpose and our values in service of who we are, our identity.

CORE PURPOSE

Your core purpose is there to help you articulate meaning – *your* meaning – so that you can use it as a compass, your north star, to keep you balanced steadily within your realm of Enough. In *Leading from Purpose*, Nick Craig offers this description: 'your purpose brings meaning to life's challenges... people who lead from purpose stick with it when no one is supporting them, and they do it anyway.'[12] Purpose resides in the state of Enough – the middle of our scales. It is drawn from within and is fundamentally true to the whole of us: what we think, what we feel, what we give ourselves permission to be and do. It is in the Art of Enough sweet spot and it is the thing that will keep you centred as you move from letting go to letting come.

You might know the story of Alfred Nobel, the man who invented the Nobel international prizes right? Well... yes and... In 1888, seven years before he died, Nobel had never thought of establishing an international prize celebrating the best of human endeavour. One morning, just after his brother had died, he sat down to his breakfast and opened the newspaper, where to his shock, he started reading his own obituary. The journalist of the Paris newspaper had mistaken his brother for him and had written an obituary of the wrong Nobel – him. The headline? 'Le marchand de la mort est mort' ('The merchant of death is dead'). Because up to that point, Alfred Nobel was famous for manufacturing and selling dynamite. He was an arms dealer. Nobel was so appalled by this being his legacy that he made a conscious choice to change it. He dedicated the rest of his life to setting up the prizes and left a majority of his wealth to this end. Now, most of us won't have such stark moments of truth as this one. But it is worth taking a moment of pause. As Mary Oliver puts it in her wonderful poem *The Summer Day*, 'Tell me, what is it you plan to do with your one wild and precious life?'[13]

Taking a really wide lens to this question can be helpful in articulating your identity and your purpose. If you zoom right out for a minute – imagining you are at the end of your working life, or to a significant birthday celebration as you get older – what is it that you would like to be appreciated for? What do you want to be known for *being*? (This is your identity.) What do you want to be known for *doing*? (This is your purpose.) This isn't about external recognition. It is about being true to who you are and giving yourself permission not just to dream it but to inhabit it at the deepest level. Daniel Pink, in *Drive: The Surprising Truth about What Motivates Us*,[14] describes his research into intrinsic motivation in which he found that 'the most deeply motivated people – not to mention those who are the most productive and satisfied – hitch their desires to a cause larger than themselves'. It can help to think of your purpose in terms of your contribution: what you are serving or giving back to the world.

 PRACTICE 8: CORE PURPOSE

1. Michelangelo reportedly said, 'The greatest danger for most of us is not that our aim is too high and we miss it, but that it is too low and we reach it.' Allow yourself the luxury of setting aside any thought of whether or not it's actually possible to live your core purpose and reside for a moment in the place of deep connection with yourself.

Now reflect on these questions:

- What is your core purpose? Let your imagination and ambition run free.
- What is your boldest, most lofty ambition for the difference or contribution you want to make to the world?
- Write it down.

2. Don't worry if what you've ended up with sounds a bit grand – think of it as the contribution that you and only you can make. For me when I did this activity, I found my purpose was: 'To support individuals, organizations and humankind to restore balance in their lives and in our world.' It made me feel a little embarrassed to write it – I began to hear imposter voices from my Scarcity Mindset – 'Who the hell do you think you are?' But the longer I sat with it, the more it felt true. So I wrote it as an action: 'I *will* support individuals, organizations and humankind to restore balance in their lives and in our world.'

   - Below your core purpose write it as an action sentence.

3. The final step is to connect your purpose with daily life, so it remains real and grounded rather than lofty and remote. For me this was, 'and I start by re-balancing myself.'
   - Add a sentence to your core purpose that links to your daily life.

Now, when I am feeling off balance, overwhelmed with a sense of Scarcity or Excess, I remind myself of my purpose and it brings me back to my felt sense of Enough. I have written it down as an action and it sits there above my desk – my purpose borne out of my identity and my sense of service. It trumps all the other voices in my head, and more than that, it *feels* right.

KNOW YOUR VALUES

Once you know your 'what', it can help to identify your 'why'. We've talked a lot about beliefs in this chapter, and your values are an articulation of these. As we know, they are yours to choose, once you have disentangled beliefs that don't belong to you and stepped away from those that don't serve your identity or your purpose.

 PRACTICE 9: VALUES

- Write down ten words that describe the things that are most important to you. What matters most to you in relation to how you want to live? If you were a stick of rock, what would it say in the middle?
- These words could be people focused (like family, friendships, community) or behaviour focused (trust, connection, creativity) or emotion focused (love, generosity). If you find this hard, there are lots of 'values lists' available on the internet that can give you a place to start.
- Once you have ten, try and whittle it down to five. The very act of selecting fewer words helps you to focus on what really is more important for you.

- Now say your name followed by 'and I believe in' before you list your values. Notice how resonant they feel. Your values can act as an inner compass and identifying them can offer great clarity.

I've found this a really useful exercise to do from time to time throughout my life – not least because I'm curious to see if they have stayed the same. What might have been really important to me when I was 25 may not hold so much potency now I've turned 50. Having said that, my values have changed surprisingly little; they are still: love, abundance, creativity, inclusivity and connection. They are fundamental to who I am and what I believe about the world and what my contribution can be – both personally and professionally. They flow out of my identity and my core purpose and shape how I live my life.

THE FREEDOM OF YOUR OWN PERMISSION

Glennon Doyle in *Untamed*[15] writes, 'What if I don't need *your* permission slip because I'm already free?' The simple act of writing down the things that you want to be able to do or be in order to fulfil your core purpose can itself give you freedom. You are re-writing your own script. In doing so, you are sourcing the approval from within, so that you don't have to rely on others to give you your sense of what being Enough is. You are re-setting your loyalties so that you are not blindly loyal to a belief that is no longer serving you: you are being loyal to a belief that will help you in the present moment.

Much of the work of this chapter has involved looking inward and looking back into your past, in order to release yourself into the present, facing the future – to move forward in ways that are fruitful and freeing for you. Writing down your permission slips for your unentangled beliefs, your purpose and your values – and then repeating these with each breath, for a few minutes each morning – can be a powerful way to help you to re-set your nervous system and give yourself Enough Permission to thrive, flourish and grow into everything you have the potential to be, so that along with Michelle Obama, you can say in all honesty: 'Am I good enough? Yes I am!'

SUMMARY OF *ENOUGH PERMISSION*

- We often carry our deepest beliefs about ourselves and the world unconsciously.
- Our beliefs and assumptions are what can hold us back most potently because they are familiar and make us feel a sense of belonging.
- Bringing our beliefs to light and working out where they came from is powerful because it gives us choice.
- Breaking old 'rules of belonging' that aren't true to us anymore can be uncomfortable but is necessary for us to change and grow.
- Once we have let go of old limiting beliefs, we are free to create our own identity, core purpose and values.
- Articulating and owning who we are, what we are here for and what matters most, will build our inner sense of being Enough.

The transformative potential within Enough Permission is...

...the freedom to be who we are

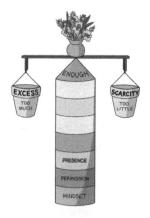

ART 3: ENOUGH PRESENCE

HOW TO MANAGE YOUR STATE TO FIND FLOW

Enough Haiku
After all is said and done
I am still here
Breathing in each moment

So far in this journey, we have explored ways to find your Art of Enough through how you think and feel. In Art 3, we are going to bring in our body, our physicality. This will involve us getting intensely practical about our neurobiology in each moment – particularly when we are under pressure and our bodies respond instinctively. It will also involve taking a good look at our energy and how it affects our presence. We'll explore how to keep aligned and connected with the whole of our bodies, and why this is so important for your state of Enough Presence.

We will look at:

- *what Enough Presence gives you;*
- *how we are programmed to respond to risk;*
- *finding Enough Presence through the heart–brain connection;*
- *using Enough Presence to harness your nerves;*
- *re-wiring your systems so you can be in the present moment;*
- *neuroplasticity – you can change how you think;*
- *getting to know your hormones and brain chemicals.*

WHAT ENOUGH PRESENCE GIVES YOU

What does Enough feel like in your body? Where do you feel it – in your head, heart or gut? These may sound like strange questions, and yet, how we experience life is hugely influenced by how we feel physically. When we think about having Enough Presence, we are exploring how we create a state of internal cohesion. This space is aligned, balanced and centred in the place of Enough moment by moment. Harvard social psychologist Amy Cuddy defines presence as, 'the state of being attuned to and able to comfortably express our true thoughts, feelings, values and potential' and that when we do, 'our speech, facial expressions, postures and movements align. They synchronize and focus. And that *internal convergence*, that harmony is palpable and

resonant – because it's real. It's what makes us compelling'
(*my italics*).[1] Enough Presence is embodying all that we have
explored so far in this book. It is both our minds and our
bodies in balance with each other – as one system working
coherently, in service of our purpose, values and potential.

I trained as an actor many moons ago, and my peers and I
spent a lot of time studying 'stage presence'. What is it about
a particular actor that makes them so compelling compared
to the other actors on the stage? What is the secret special
'something' about their energy? We could ask the same set of
questions about anyone. What is it that gives some leaders,
politicians, sports people or some friends or work colleagues
in our social groups that elusive but oh so magnetic quality
– presence? I came to learn during my training and work as
an actor that presence is the ability to inhabit the present
moment fully. When you are acting, you are in a state of
suspended animation – fully immersed in the fusion of
yourself and your character – so entirely in the moment that
any other thought or distraction will knock you off balance.
It requires intense focus, concentration and energy. You need
to be so proficient in what you are doing that you don't have
to concentrate on it, leaving you free to use your energy to
connect to the present moment and those around you.

Presence isn't just important for actors of course; it
matters to all of us – we all need to be present to our lives and
connect with others. We want to be able to be our authentic
selves in each moment and for people to see who we really
are, not a version of us that is distracted by anxiety or tension
or anything else that might be diverting us from what we are
doing then and there. Psychologist Mihaly Csikszentmihalyi
called this 'flow' – when we are so absorbed and focused
on the present moment that time seems to fly by.[2] We are

entirely committed to what we are doing. The gift of this practice is that it is not only absorbing and productive – it can create a state of joy. Everything is connected and aligned within you. You feel, really feel, that you are Enough, and that is transmitted to those around you. This is what Enough Presence delivers for us.

If you are anything like me though, you might sometimes just wake up feeling a bit 'off', and then struggle to feel anything like balance or Enough for reasons that you simply can't put your finger on. On these days, I may have done my regular practices for finding Enough with my mindset and my feelings but still just feel not quite right in my gut – or perhaps just a bit anxious or simply unable to stop my brain from over-thinking. I am in a place of Scarcity or sometimes Excess and I can't seem to re-balance. Alternatively, I may be having a great day, completely on top of my game, and then something triggers me to lose balance. This could be a request to do something that I find stressful, or the way someone speaks to me, and my entire way of being changes. It's on these days and in these moments that we need to explore our physiology and understand how the Art of Enough manifests in our *state*. We can then identify what is going on in our bodies – in our heads, hearts and guts – and learn practices to bring us back to a state of equilibrium, back into now.

Looking again at our Art of Enough model, Enough is the place of balance, abundance, freedom and belonging, poised between a place of Scarcity (fear, lack, anxiety) and Excess (overwhelm, addiction, desire); the state of Enough Presence is how we *feel* our way into finding this balance from the inside out. It really is a physical state, aided, of course, by the work we've done on mindset and permission. Our physiology is a highly dynamic system – changing moment by moment, breath by breath, heartbeat by heartbeat – so we need to know what our bodies are hard-wired to do. Let's explore how our instinctive physiological responses can trip us up and look at ways to get ourselves into a state of Enough.

'BE CAREFUL!' HOW WE ARE PROGRAMMED TO RESPOND TO RISK

When our second daughter was a toddler learning to walk up and down stairs, she used to take one step at a time and say with each step, 'Careful! Careful! Careful!' (Nothing to do with us being particularly cautious parents – our other daughter bounced up and down them with kamikaze abandon!) I always think of this in relation to how our bodies function. Our brains are hard-wired to keep us safe and to protect us from any perceived risk. Consequently, our brains are significantly more sensitive to picking up cues that are negative – anything that might be potentially dangerous – than positive ones.

Our ability to perceive and react quickly to risk is, of course, what has kept us homo sapiens safe for centuries. It was key to our survival when we were living with very real life-threatening dangers every day in hunter-gatherer communities in the wild. However, now that we are not having to navigate life and death risks daily, we have to learn instead how to manage our risk responses. As trauma clinician Peter Levine puts it, 'though most of us no longer dwell in caves, we retain an intense expectation of lurking danger, be it from others of our own species or from predators… Such paralysing fearfulness has outlasted its survival utility in humans. Such intractable fear prevents a person from returning to balance and normal life.[3] Ironically, stress is now a bigger killer than the risks our bodies are hard-wired to defend us against. More people in the twenty-first century die of stress-related illness than are being killed by wild animals. We now need to be vigilant about our own vigilance, in order to protect ourselves. If we were computers, we'd be running a really old operating system, and like computers, we sometimes need to give ourselves a software update. When we learn practices of being present, we find that we have a lot of power to change our responses. In doing so, we give ourselves so much more choice in life.

What is going on in our bodies then, in those moments when we need to be on top of our game, but somehow get pushed out of Enough Presence into something much more like real fear? If, like me, you have ever frozen in the middle of speaking when giving a talk or presentation, if you have ever over-reacted to something someone has said and lashed out in anger, and if you have ever wanted to run away and hide under a duvet when things got stressful, then welcome to the human race! We are built to react in this way to danger, and these are the impulses we really need to understand, so that we can actively learn how to calm our systems and re-set. We'll start by looking at the more immediate fear triggers, and then take a look at some of the other fear patterns at play in our bodies. It turns out that the place we need to look at in our body system first in order to understand how we respond to risk is not our brains at all, but the centre of our physicality – most commonly associated with emotion and life force – our heart. This will require us to put our biology heads on for a minute – but it is really worth understanding how our physical system works, because in doing so we give ourselves freedom to find our balance and presence in the moments that matter.

FINDING ENOUGH PRESENCE THROUGH THE HEART–BRAIN CONNECTION

Understanding the heart and the impact it has on the way our brains work informs how we can manage our state moment by moment. It genuinely holds the key to returning to our Enough Presence when we are under pressure. Let's start with some interesting facts about the heart. It is the biggest muscle in our body and beats about 100,000 times a day. It is auto rhythmic, which means that it doesn't depend on a signal from the brain in order to beat. In fact, the heart sends more signals to the brain than the other way around and it has a bigger impact on the way we think than you might expect – especially in relation to how we detect risk. The way our heart is beating at any given time sends a message to the brain telling it whether we are in danger or not.

The HeartMath Institute has been researching the significance of how the heart beats and the impact it has on the brain for years.[4] Doc Childre and Deborah Rozman describe this in detail in *Transforming Stress: The HeartMath Solution for Relieving Worry, Fatigue and Tension*.[5] They found the heart is the first part of the body to respond to perceived danger. The heart sends a message to the brain, which in turn triggers a threat response, not the other way around, as is commonly thought. This is important because it changes what we focus on when managing our stress responses. We can understand what sort of message the heart is sending to the brain by looking at our heart rate variability – commonly referred to by the initials HRV.

Our HRV is the distance between each heartbeat. Our heart does not beat entirely mechanistically like a metronome. The heartbeat is variable precisely because we need our heart muscle to be elastic, so that it can beat fast when we need it to (when we run for a bus, for example) and it can slow down when we need it to (when we are relaxing). We want to have a high HRV because it shows that our heart has the capacity to speed up or slow down – it's elastic enough for life's different circumstances. When we measure our HRV over a few minutes, we get a trace – think of the machine that people get hooked up to in hospital with the little beep…beep…beep. This trace can show us the pattern of the HRV – and in turn can tell us whether our heart is beating *coherently* or not. And it is this coherence that is critical to our brain's response. If our HRV is *coherent*, it shows a smooth trace.

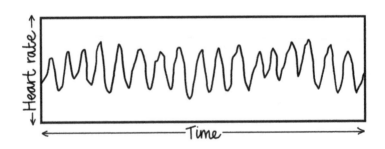

If it is beating *incoherently*, the trace looks different – I liken it to the Three Musketeers being in high alert – ready for a fight – 'en garde!'

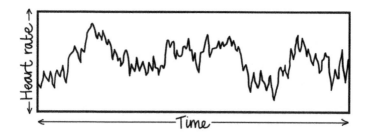

Imagine these two traces above as being a ride in a taxi: which car would you rather be travelling in? There's the smooth, gentle ride of coherence, or the stop, start, juddery ride of incoherence. If our heart is beating coherently, the message it sends to our brain is that everything is ok. There is no risk to be worrying about. On the other hand, when our heart starts to beat incoherently, the opposite happens. It sends a message to the brain that we are in danger.

When the heart starts to beat incoherently, it triggers a part of our brain called the amygdala. The amygdala is a small area situated right in the middle of what's known as the limbic brain (sometimes referred to as the 'chimp brain'). It is shaped like an almond (hence its name, derived from Ancient Greek) and sits on the hippocampus, which is the part of our brains that forms and stores memories. It may be small but it's highly significant, because it is the part of our brain that controls our immediate reaction to danger. Think of the amygdala as our crisis response centre. When it gets triggered, it absorbs a lot of the brain's energy and overrides other areas of the brain. I think of it like a toddler having a tantrum, jumping up and down and demanding attention, which it gets. The other parts of our brain fade into insignificance and the amygdala offers us three options: fight, flight or freeze.

In *Emotional Intelligence*,[6] Daniel Goleman coined the term 'amygdala hijack' and that is what it feels like – we are hijacked – out of control of our response, at the mercy of our instinct to protect ourselves. When the amygdala is triggered, we produce the hormones adrenaline and cortisol (more of which later) and we respond – like all other mammals – with the instinct to either fight, to run away as fast as we can, or to stay as still as we can so that we are not spotted by whatever is putting us in danger. This is really helpful if we are about to be attacked by a bear, or even if we are crossing a road and hadn't seen a bus coming. We don't want our brain in those moments to spend any wasted time thinking about things that aren't fundamental to our survival. As the bus that we haven't seen approaches, we don't want to be thinking, 'I wish I'd worn better shoes for running – should I take these ones off, or shall I just risk the blister?!' We just want everything to react together – 'RUN!' – in this way, we keep ourselves safe. However, it is significantly less helpful if our amygdala is triggered when we are just about to have an important conversation with someone about something that really matters. Or if we are about to speak in public. Or someone says something in a meeting that undermines our point. At those moments, fighting, running away or freezing are the opposite of helpful. In those moments, we want an area of our brain called the 'pre-frontal cortex' to be in charge.

The pre-frontal cortex is just underneath our foreheads at the front of our skull. Sometimes referred to as 'the human brain', it is the bit of our brain that we do not share with our closest primate cousins. It's associated with decision making, language, goal setting, sense-making, planning and problem solving – all things that make us think well and clearly. It is like the executive function of the brain. David Rock in *Your Brain at Work*[7] describes the pre-frontal cortex as, 'the biological seat of your conscious interactions with the world. It's… central to thinking things through, instead of being on "autopilot" as you go about your life.' It is in charge of how we think as humans.

When the amygdala is triggered, as we've established, all other parts of the brain, including our pre-frontal cortex, cede attention to the more urgent requirement of keeping us safe. When the heart starts to beat incoherently, sending a message to the brain that we are in danger, the energy in the brain leaves the pre-frontal cortex and centres around the amygdala and our instinctive responses.

What can we do in those moments to move us away from the immediacy of reacting – and re-gain Enough Presence? Remember, it is your heart that has triggered this response by starting to beat incoherently. The quickest way to get your pre-frontal cortex back in control and to politely invite the amygdala to stand down and keep quiet is to focus on your heart and get it to beat coherently again. How do we do that? Well, by using our breath. When we breathe really deeply into our abdominal area, filling our lungs with a lot of air, the heart responds by assuming that if we have time to do that, we can't be in danger, so it starts to beat coherently again. Actually, it takes on average three to five deep breaths to restore the heartbeat back to coherence. If you want to, you can also send your attention and energy to your heart, so that you are consciously helping it to know that you are not in danger. We are re-connecting our bodies with our brains, breathing our way back into coherence. Our whole physiological system is connected and highly attuned. The breath calms the heart, which changes how it beats and what message it sends to the brain, which changes whether our brain perceives we are at risk or not.

 PRACTICE 10: COHERENT BREATHING

Here's a summary of the coherent breathing technique for you. It's deliberately an 'eyes open in the moment' technique, so that you can use it any time you notice you are having an amygdala hijack.

- Focus on your heart area – you are deliberately focusing on your heart beating coherently. The simple distraction of moving your attention to something other than risk is also a good technique to over-ride the amygdala response.
- Take a deep inhale to the count of five, and then exhale to the count of five. You should be able to feel your breath in your abdomen, so your lungs are full. The reason for breathing in and out to the same count is that you are trying to activate a state of active calm. If you are feeling panicky, extending your out breath for longer will activate your 'rest and digest' response.
- Repeat this breathing pattern for up to five breaths, or as long as you can. No one need ever know you are doing it, but it will transform how you can respond in the moment. By restoring your heart to coherence, you are once more fully equipped to engage with what is required of you.

- This is an incredibly useful tool to have at your disposal. Practise it every day, so that you can access it quickly in the moments you need it.

As in Arts 1 and 2, the trick is self-awareness – notice, notice, notice. It's important to learn to notice that you are having an amygdala hijack. How? Well, the tell-tale signs come, surprise, surprise, from other clues held in your body. You might have a dry mouth, become hot and sweaty (hands and neck especially), you might feel your heart pounding, shake, or have tension in your abdominal area. Or you might just become lost for words, or so angry that you can't focus on what you were trying to say, or just want to cry or run and hide. Start to notice whether your response is emotional or physical. And then breathe. Deep, regular coherent breathing. Eyes wide open, in the moment, and let your heart do the rest. The wonderful thing about this is that you can do this at the very moment you need to recover. You don't need to leave the room and meditate for 20 minutes – you can stay in that meeting, under that spotlight, in that difficult conversation and breathe your way back into Enough Presence there and then. One of my coaching clients, Hina, described what happened when she used this technique during a conversation she had been dreading.

> It was amazing; I was in a state of panic and just couldn't get my words out. I remembered to start to breathe properly, and within a couple of minutes I got my focus back. I felt calm and really clear. Like everything just clicked back into place in that very moment.

When I work with people on their HRV and teach the breathing and coherence techniques, the thing that most surprises them is that their HRV changes so quickly. We can move from incoherence to coherence and back again within a matter of seconds. Our physiology is an amazingly highly tuned balancing system – constantly adjusting, reacting to whatever signals it receives. When we think of our Enough Presence, we need to remember that it, too, is highly dynamic. We don't just get into a state of Enough and then stay there for the day. We shift and change moment by moment – and the Art of Enough is about acknowledging this fact and being alert to the need to re-balance time and again throughout the day.

USING ENOUGH PRESENCE TO HARNESS YOUR NERVES

There are moments for all of us in our lives when we really need whatever it is we are doing to go well. These moments of high performance (whether they are high-octane work moments or really crucial personal ones) often make us feel nervous and hyped up. This is normal. It actually gives you the energy you need for the task ahead of you. The technique of breathing to calm your heart is a way of harnessing your nerves and energy, rather than letting them trip you up. It's the difference between finding flow and having an amygdala hijack.

Back to acting, the years of theatre touring I did taught me how to prepare for being in the state of Enough. Before every single show, the entire company would meet on stage two hours before curtain-up and do a physical warm-up together. We would limber up our bodies and our voices of course, and we would also do breathing exercises, very similar to the coherent breathing I've outlined here. It doesn't matter if your heart is beating faster than normal – that is appropriate for high performance. What matters is that it is coherent (remember the smooth curves of the coherent heart trace). Deep, even breathing puts us into a state of active calm – alert and ready to give our best in the moment. We harness our nerves rather than let them hijack us because we are in a state of Enough Presence, described by voice coach Patsy Rodenburg as: 'the energy that comes from you and connects you to the outside world. It is essential to your survival when you are threatened. It is the heart of intimacy between people… It is when you are fully present that you do your best work and make your deepest impression.'[8]

Like anything, the more you can practise this technique so that you have it to hand when you need it most, the better. Along with the content of anything you are planning to do, practise the state you want to be in too. Learning to keep your heart coherent will help you build the ability to re-set your Enough Presence, so that you are not reacting to challenges from a place of instinctive survival, but from a conscious state of awareness. Perhaps it should come as no surprise that for us to live our lives from a state of Enough, balanced in the place of abundance and flow – away from fear, anxiety, overwhelm and scarcity – we need to focus on our hearts: the symbol of love and connection.

RE-WIRING YOUR SYSTEMS SO YOU CAN BE IN THE PRESENT MOMENT

We've talked so far about the importance and impact of being present, and of some of the immediate physical triggers that might get in the way. I've often wondered why being present (and therefore Enough Presence) is such a struggle for us human beings. Philosopher Alan Watts suggests: 'Our primary mode of relinquishing presence is by leaving the body and retreating into the mind – that ever-calculating, self-evaluating, seething cauldron of thoughts, predictions, anxieties and judgements.'[9] When we lose our presence, we can get caught up in habits of thought, which can make us feel anxious or overwhelmed. For spiritual teacher Eckhart Tolle, it is the compulsion to focus on the past (worry, regret, over-analysing events, rumination) or the pull of the future (anxiety, planning, control) that takes us away from the present moment.[10]

The ability to be alert in the present moment takes practice and skill – and it's an essential part of each of us finding the Art of Enough. It requires us, once again, to notice what is going on for us, so that we can learn to identify when we are not in a state of balance and learn how to bring ourselves back. There is a growing body of evidence demonstrating the benefits of meditating and mindfulness on increasing our brain and body function and the ability to remain coherent. Significantly, research has found that the structure of the brain changes as a result of regular mindfulness and breathing practice – particularly in the pre-frontal cortex area. You may remember that this is the part of our brain where we do our most intensive human thinking. These changes include an increase in the attention span, increased body awareness, emotional regulation and change in perspective on ourselves. It would seem that we can literally train ourselves to build our Enough Presence by adopting a regular daily practice – whether it's box breathing, mindfulness, meditation or yoga. Whatever you pick, there are many wonderful resources available and I recommend that you find a regular practice that helps you to build your capacity to be present and in the moment.

This is the tip of the iceberg of exploring our physiological make-up and how we respond somatically. For now though, I want to zoom in on just two more significant aspects of the way our bodies work that can really help us to build up our Enough Presence: neuroplasticity and our hormones. Learning about these two things has transformed the practices that I use and offer to my clients. It's been incredibly effective in supporting them to create and maintain a state of being Enough and living a richer, fuller life.

NEUROPLASTICITY – YOU CAN CHANGE HOW YOU THINK

Neuroplasticity is such a useful and hopeful discovery to have come from all the fMRI scanning and brain research in recent years. Neuroplasticity is a long word to describe the fact that our brains change and grow all the time, and as such we can change how we think. Our brains are full of neurons which connect when we think something, forming what is called a neural pathway. An early neuroscientist, Donald Hebb, came up with what is now known as Hebb's Principle in 1949: 'neurons that fire together, wire together';[11] the more we think about something, the stronger that neural pathway becomes in our brains. Imagine that you wake up on a snowy day and walk across an untouched field of fresh snow. It makes a small path. Over the day, others walk the same path until by the evening, it is quite established. Neural pathways are like that. The more we think something, the stronger the pathway, meaning that it is easier for us to think the same thing another time. This is the way that we learn, remember things, grow. It also means that we can change the way our brain is wired if we choose to – we just need to repeat our thinking and create a new neural pathway.

Evidence of neuroplasticity was found by Professor Eleanor Maguire, a scientist from UCL, who studied a group of applicants to become London black cab drivers (cabbies) before and after they undertook the famous 'Knowledge' exam to qualify.[12] Notoriously hard, the Knowledge takes an average of three years to study for and requires future cabbies to learn up to 18,000 routes across the city. The fMRI scans of potential cabbies showed that those who passed the exam had increased the size of their posterior hippocampus – the part of the brain associated with working memory and spatial awareness. Doing the Knowledge literally changed the shape of their brains: their working memory grew bigger.

Neuroplasticity demonstrates that we all have the potential to change how we think. We can change the structure of our brains by creating new neural pathways. Positive psychologists have been talking about this for many years. In *Learned Optimism*,[13] Martin Seligman was the first of many after him to outline how we can create an alternative story to any negative thinking pattern we might have. Say your regular response to making a mistake is, 'Typical, I always get things wrong.' This is a negative neural pathway that has built up through frequent use over many years. However, it can be countered if we can create an equally strong alternative: a positive neural pathway, such as, 'What can I learn from this?' With practice, we can develop this thinking pattern so that we are giving our brain a choice of which neural pathway to take. The old one doesn't disappear, but the more we use the new pathway the stronger and more established it becomes. The less we use the old one, the less pronounced it will be, until eventually, our brains physically change shape and create a new pattern.

It's not just patterns of thought that make neuroplasticity such an important thing to know about. It can affect how we feel and respond too – we are integrated systems, after all. For example, imagine having butterflies in your tummy. Sometimes they signify nerves, and other times (think of a five-year-old child before their birthday) they signify excitement. It's the same physiological response to two quite different events. This can be used to our advantage. If you get butterflies before you do something you are nervous about – such as taking a flight – your brain might react with a fear pattern, which in turn triggers other fear responses in our bodies. However, as it is the exact same physiological response that happens in your abdomen when you are excited, you can train yourself to replace 'I'm scared of flying' with 'I'm excited about flying.' The butterflies won't change, but how your brain labels and interprets them does. And this in turn creates a different hormonal response in your body, which can make all the difference. Let's look at how.

GET TO KNOW YOUR HORMONES AND BRAIN CHEMICALS

Understanding how hormones and brain chemicals (technical term 'neurotransmitters') work can profoundly help us to manage and build our Enough Presence. You may have heard of some of them already, and if not, let me introduce you to just some of the cast of players:

- **Dopamine** is a reward chemical – it is released when we achieve something. It is associated with motivation; when it is activated, we feel positive and when it is depressed, we feel less good. We activate dopamine by doing something as simple as ticking something off our to-do list or completing a project we've been working on.

- **Serotonin** is sometimes called the happy hormone. When it is released, it makes us feel positive. The amount of serotonin we have in our bodies is increased by eating certain foods, after exercise, a good night's sleep, or after sitting in the sunshine.
- **Oxytocin** is released when we feel love, connection and trust. It's all about bonding. When you give someone a hug, you will get a hit of oxytocin. It can make you feel more empathic, connected and trusting of those around you.

When we consciously do things to release dopamine, serotonin and oxytocin, we can help ourselves to over-ride some of the fear-based brain responses and give ourselves instead a feeling of achievement, connection and love. This is the chemistry of Enough, and it can be used to build up our state and presence.

CORTISOL AND DHEA

Now, we're going to turn to two more hormones that make a big difference to our embodiment of Enough – cortisol and DHEA. We'll start with cortisol. Cortisol is a steroid hormone that is secreted by the adrenal glands just above our kidneys. We are moving focus here to the 'gut' area of our bodies, reminding us how important integrating the head, heart and gut can be. Cortisol has a major impact on how our bodies respond to stress. In fact, it is often called the 'stress hormone' and is the hormone that can get us trapped into a negative spiral moving between Scarcity and Excess.

Cortisol, when it is released, can be connected with good stress – we all get a burst of it when we get up in the morning, and it helps us to have a sense of energy for the day. It is released, along with adrenaline, when our amygdala is triggered. It gives us the energy we need for the fight, flight, freeze part. Again, if we are in real danger, this is appropriate and useful. According to Amy Brahn in *Neuroscience for Coaches*,[13] it gives us 'a burst of energy, heightened memory functions, lower sensitivity to pain and elevated blood pressure', meaning that we can do what we need to keep ourselves safe. If we are in danger, we *want* a flood of cortisol – a big burst of it flushes through our system and clears itself out.

However, the reason cortisol gets so much bad press is that many of us live with constantly elevated levels of it, which can build up over time, and cortisol takes a long time to metabolize. In this form, when it is not associated with real and present danger but longer-term enduring stress, it stays in our systems for longer – and it doesn't go away. Worse still, it has a negative impact on our bodies – it breaks things down, including the connectors in our brain. High levels of cortisol can make it hard for us to sleep (it's a stimulant), and tiredness means that our bodies produce more cortisol (to keep us alert). It can also affect mood, appetite and, more seriously, has been connected in numerous medical studies with long-term and life-threatening illnesses. So far, so gloomy.

In the interests of using this information to find Enough Presence, let's explore things which help us reduce our levels of unwanted cortisol. The HeartMath Institute teaches that cortisol works like a see-saw with another hormone produced in our adrenal glands, commonly known as DHEA (dehydroepiandrosterone). If we have high levels of cortisol, we have lower levels of DHEA and vice versa. DHEA is one of the few things that metabolizes cortisol and as such, it helps us get rid of unwanted cortisol in our systems. And here's the really good news: DHEA is produced when we feel positive. This is where it merges into a practice that we can adopt to help us actively encourage a reward response in our bodies to build our Enough Presence. We can stimulate DHEA by making ourselves feel happy.

PRACTICE 11: POSITIVITY PORTFOLIO

Creating DHEA can become a practice – and to do so, I often invite people I'm working with to build a 'positivity portfolio'.

- Think of three things (people, places, memories) that are guaranteed to make you smile, and write them down. These don't have to be big, grand events; they can be ordinary things. To quote Kent Nerburn, 'We dream our lives in grand gestures, but we live our lives in small moments'.[14] You can choose something big like your wedding day or a daily activity like my personal favourite – running along the river with my dog Wilf. It could be remembering the satisfaction you felt after completing a really difficult project or the smell of a beautiful rose. It really doesn't matter what it is, as long as it is true for you, and takes you back both to the memory and feeling of what you are thinking about. The test for this is that it automatically brings a smile to your lips.

- Once you have a list in your portfolio, the simple act of practising to think of them will help you create useful neural pathways in your brain. Practise bringing them to mind every day.
- Another way to build your positivity portfolio is by keeping a gratitude journal. At the end of the day, note down three things that you have appreciated or feel grateful for. This practice gets you in the habit of routinely noticing what you appreciate in each moment or each day and, over time, trains your brain to do so automatically.

Like anything that requires skill, practising really does help. It can be hard to think of something that makes you happy when you are full of cortisol, feeling stressed or frazzled. Without practice, you are unlikely to be able to think about a beautiful sunset with your significant other when you are screaming with road rage at a T-junction. However, when you practise thinking about your positivity portfolio every day, you create a strong neural pathway for this thought pattern, so that it becomes quickly accessible to you when you need it. You are training yourself to think about things that will help you, in the moment, to release hormones which over-ride a sense of Excess or Scarcity and bring you into a state of love, abundance and appreciation – Enough Presence.

The Art of Enough

ENOUGH PRESENCE

Finding Enough Presence is as delicate and responsive as a dial on a compass. How we show up in each moment counts. It is as much about being as it is doing – and doing is from a place of coherence. In this chapter, we have delved a lot into neurobiology in order to learn how important it is to have a holistic sense of our body working as one system in balance. We have focused on the heart (HRV), brain (amygdala and neuroplasticity) and the gut (hormones created in the adrenal glands). The head, heart and gut are sometimes called our 'three brains'. All three are connected by the nervous system and when we are in a state of Enough Presence, they will communicate coherently – highly attuned to respond to one another so that we can operate in a state of flow. When we learn to trust our gut instinct, understand that our heart has a crucial function in us feeling balanced, and that our brains are not the only part of us that control our responses, we can build an embodiment of Enough which helps us flourish.

SUMMARY OF *ENOUGH PRESENCE*

- Your state – how you are in every moment – is key to building your sense of being Enough.
- Learning how to connect your physiology with your thoughts and beliefs will help you to manage each moment.
- Understanding how your body responds to pressure and stress gives you the keys to manage your response.
- Your heart is your body's risk centre. To manage how you respond to stress, learn how to make your heart beat coherently.

- Deep breathing is key to coherence, and will help you stay in the present moment.
- Feeling positive triggers hormones that combat stress: practise bringing to mind positive thoughts and feelings.

The transformative potential within Enough Presence is...

...finding flow

PART 2

THE ART OF *DOING* ENOUGH

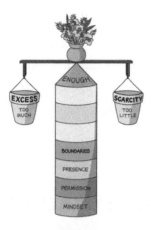

ART 4: ENOUGH BOUNDARIES

THE CLARITY OF COHERENCE

What is this life if, full of care,
We have no time to stand and stare.

W.H. Davies[1]

The globalized digital world we live in is so full of possibilities,
choices and freedoms that our ancestors never experienced –
and it is also massively complex. To live well in such complexity,
we need to find a way of giving ourselves structure so that we do
Enough: not too much or too little. We need boundaries – good

boundaries – to contain and enable us to find the Art of Enough so that we can flourish. Art 4 looks specifically at:

- *the importance of acknowledging what is;*
- *24/7 demands: from clear lines to complexity;*
- *murmurations: nature's coherent boundaries;*
- *identifying what matters most;*
- *understanding your energy patterns;*
- *designing your days, protecting your focus and saying no;*
- *the joy of Enough Boundaries.*

THE IMPORTANCE OF ACKNOWLEDGING WHAT IS

Amani's voice is full of tension and exhaustion. She is describing the demands on her life. Amani works full time as an English teacher, a demanding job so she's used to working hard, but she's telling me this feels somehow different. We are talking during the first long lockdown of Covid-19 and the global pandemic has amplified pressure on many people who are now working from home. Amani has a lot of work to do – committed as she is to her students who she is now teaching online. She has the added pressure of having to home-school her nine- and seven-year-old children while their schools are shut. And she is providing remote care for her mother, who is frail and vulnerable and lives two hundred miles away – in the form of daily calls, organising shopping and liaising with her care givers. As part of her institution's senior management team, she also attends regular meetings online in the late afternoon, the actions of which she will do later in the evening once the kids are in bed. She is getting up earlier and earlier to attend to her emails before she sorts her children out and starts her working day. Amani has never worked so hard and she feels wrung out. At the end of our call she wails, 'I feel like I'm being pulled in all directions and I'm doing everything badly. I feel guilty the whole time that I should be doing something else, and I'm exhausted. It's just… impossible!'

Amani is right. What she is being asked to do is impossible. She simply cannot do it all. She has too much to do. It is genuinely overwhelming. Her energy is depleted from having kept up this pace for many weeks and she is in danger of running out of resource. I invite Amani to just say to herself: 'It's impossible' a few times until it really sinks in. After about the fifth time of saying it out loud, she exclaims, as if she has finally realized deep down what she is really saying and hearing it for the first time:

'It *is* though! It actually *is* IMPOSSIBLE!'

Yup. What she is demanding of herself and what is being demanded of her is too much and unsustainable at this pace.

'So, what the hell can I do about it?'

Thinking about Enough Permission, I invited Amani to consider, 'Who are you being loyal to?' and 'Who are you really trying to please here?'

Acknowledging that 'it is impossible' is the first, very important step in helping Amani to move from where she is, to a better place. She can only do what she has the energy to do in the time she has and no more. And until she stops trying to do more than is physically possible, she will only ever fall short. While both time and energy are renewable, they require space and attention in order to renew.

There is a big difference between agreeing *with* something and agreeing that it is true. We're not saying we like it; we are just being honest about the reality. The simple act of naming and acknowledging things just as they are has a great power to it. By necessity it is an inclusive act. Everything that contributes to things being just as they are is laid bare and included. Once Amani had agreed that the demands on her life were more than she could physically continue to do long term, she was able to see things as they were. Remember that it took her some time to reach this realization. Just saying 'It's impossible!' once wasn't enough – she had to repeat it with resonance to let the truth of it drop into her body, so she felt the truth of it deeply within her consciousness. This gave her a starting point for change as she tuned into her state of Enough Presence.

When she had acknowledged the truth of her situation, stepped back and looked at the whole, she realized that she did have some choices about how she was living. She couldn't change the demands on her, but she could choose how she responded. It was down to *her* to make choices which would give her clarity and agency to move forward. For Amani, and indeed any of us who have experienced feeling overwhelmed by the volume and complexity of what there is to do, remembering that we have freedom to make some choices, however small, is a really important place to start.

Amani's story is a familiar one. Change her setting and context and nearly everyone I have ever worked with or spoken to about this issue will have experienced a version of this conundrum at some time in their lives. Covid-19 has exacerbated the situation felt for years by many, which is the perceived requirement to be always on, always available and responsive. In lockdown, the boundaries between work and home were more blurred than ever, and because of the schools being shut, parents and carers were having to juggle the demands of caregiving, home schooling and work. People experienced 'working from home' as 'living at work' – they simply couldn't get away from the pressures.

24/7 DEMANDS: FROM CLEAR LINES TO COMPLEXITY

Even before the global pandemic, working within boundaries was an increasing challenge for people. Twenty-four/seven digital availability is by definition boundaryless – and those with large volumes of work and multiple pressures can struggle to switch off. When you are holding a lot of responsibility and juggling multiple requirements, commitments and demands from different places, whether they come from work, home or simply your own inner voice, it can feel impossible to draw the line – and indeed to draw breath. No one will tell you not to send a tweet at midnight or check your emails before you've even got out of bed in the morning. That's on you.

In our Art of Enough model, we move like a see-saw between Excess – the fact of having too much to do, and Scarcity – the fact that we don't have enough time and resource. And then, because we don't feel that we are doing enough (Scarcity again), we don't let ourselves stop (Excess) – and so the see-sawing continues. The gathering sense of pace and urgency that accompanies this movement is usually an indication that we are working from the left hemisphere of our brain: the part which operates our logic and planning.

We are probably in a 'head' state not a 'heart' state, which can exacerbate the sense of running out of time. We can become disconnected from our bodies when we are working at pace in this way. How can we stop the swing and find balance so that we can rest at the point of Enough? A good place to start, once we've acknowledged the situation, is by creating some boundaries of our own.

One of the reasons that creating boundaries can be so challenging in our digital age is that we have to set them ourselves. Gone are the days when boundaries were set by the organizations and society people worked and lived in. The twentieth-century working paradigm was typified by Henry Ford's production line. This was a mechanistic and structured approach to work. Most people had clear times to start and end work. Think nine to five, whether it was in an office, factory or trade. Work productivity was measured in terms of units of time. 'Time is money' became the refrain, and subsequently working long hours, for some, became a badge of honour – a symbol of ultimate commitment and increased productivity. As a majority of people worked outside of the home, their work was measured in terms of input: how many hours they spent doing it. In my first office job in the late 1990s, I was advised that if I wanted to do well, I should be at my desk early and leave after most people had gone. Sure enough, the director of my department used these times of the day to 'walk the floor' and talk to the people that for her demonstrated the most commitment by still being there.

In the twenty-first century, we find ourselves in a very different world. People work in all sorts of ways. Some still have regular hours for work, but everyone has access to the internet and email when they get home. Many of us work from home (a trend accelerated by Covid-19) or have portfolio careers and multiple jobs or clients. For lots of people, work is measured not in terms of input but output: the results of our labour being more important than how long it takes to do something. This has been a liberation for many. It has enabled flexible working, which has allowed them to juggle work with other commitments.

However, the cost of our enhanced choice and flexibility is a lack of certainty and containment – there has been a dissolving of clarity, especially around work boundaries. Those clean lines are simply not there anymore in our VUCA world (VUCA being an acronym used to describe twenty-first-century living, which stands for volatile, uncertain, complex and ambiguous). The responsibility to create clear boundaries has shifted from others to ourselves: it requires us to impose our own structure. And if we don't create our own boundaries, we risk not having any. If we are living in a boundaryless way, more often than not we can feel uncontained and overwhelmed.

For us to live a life of Enough, we need to find a different way of thinking about boundaries for our life, and our relationship with work. We need to move away from the outdated mechanistic production line, 'time is money' approach, and towards something that helps us thrive in our complex world. As Peter Senge writes, 'reality is made up of circles, but we see straight lines.'[2] It's time to find a model for creating boundaries based on systems that thrive in complexity. Where better to look for such a model than the natural environment, itself full of self-organising, complex adaptive systems. How do nature's complex systems remain contained and coherent?

MURMURATIONS: NATURE'S COHERENT BOUNDARIES

Have you ever had the joy of seeing a murmuration of starlings? Their wonderful collective noun is taken from the rustling sound of thousands of birds' wings flying at the same time. The last time I saw one, I had just arrived in Brighton on the UK's south coast, in the early evening. I was exhausted from a demanding day followed by a long drive, and the preoccupation of my work with a client the following morning. I was in the middle of what I sometimes call euphemistically a 'busy patch' – where I follow a well-worn pattern of overcommitting and overwork. All self-imposed and driven by a genuine love of what I do but, nonetheless, too much. As I walked along the seafront from the car park to the hotel, I noticed the birds. Drawn to them, I walked to the beach and spent the next hour marvelling at the simple beauty, coherence and magnitude of thousands of birds flying in harmony over the sea as the sun was setting. The irony that I use this image as a metaphor for finding boundaries in a complex working life was not lost on me as I stood there, exhausted by overwork and exhilarated by the sight of a coherent system. Nonetheless, it was a good reminder and certainly salve for my soul that evening.

If you ever get the opportunity to go and see a murmuration, I highly recommend it. They fly at dawn and dusk in the winter and usually frequent the same places. If not, there is plenty of footage on the internet: give yourself a treat and watch one now. As you watch, you too may well marvel at how it is possible for so many birds to fly in such apparent harmony. How on earth do they fly in such astonishing formations – looking like the most stunningly choreographed dance? It is in fact a perfect example of a complex adaptive system. Murmurations work as a result of all the individual birds following three, simple 'defining principles' of behaviour. These are:

- Fly at the same speed as surrounding birds.
- Fly in the direction of the birds around you.
- Avoid collisions with other birds.

These three rules were modelled by an early complexity theorist called Craig Reynolds, who created a simulation of the birds on a computer program (wryly called 'boids') and found that this was really all that was required in order to re-create the murmuration. *Fly fast, follow another bird, don't crash.*

The lesson from these complex adaptive systems is that when a system has three defining principles or rules, it becomes able to flow – responsive, flexible and coherent. The rules release the system to be incredible. Margaret Wheatley puts it like this: 'Perhaps the most illuminating paradox of all is that the two forces that we have placed in opposition to one another – freedom and order – turn out to be partners in generating healthy, well-ordered systems.'[3] Healthy boundaries are what allow the system to flourish.

Taking a murmuration of starlings as our model for our lives, what rules could help us to live and work so that we are able to be responsive, adaptable and remain coherent? These are the rules – let's call them 'Enough Boundaries' – that will provide containment and clarity for us so that we can achieve extraordinary things. If you think in terms of non-negotiables – things that you absolutely adhere to – what three clear boundaries could you put in place to allow you to live the life you want to live? While the focus here is on you as an individual, it is, of course, important for teams and organizations to think about healthy boundaries too, and this work is just as applicable in a wider context.

The rest of this chapter will offer ideas, techniques and research that will help you to create your own Enough Boundaries so that you can flourish in complexity rather than be overwhelmed by it. When you think of your outer life as a system, in the same way that you think of your inner life (physiology) as a system, these Enough Boundaries can give you the coherence and flow you need in order to reach your potential.

Over the years of creating Enough Boundaries in this way, I have found that it can be helpful to work out what our boundaries are, by using these three categories as a starting point:

1. Identifying what matters most.
2. Understanding your energy patterns.
3. Designing your days, protecting your focus and saying no.

We'll explore these, and there will be space at the end of each category for you to think about what your Enough Boundary could be.

1. IDENTIFYING WHAT MATTERS MOST

Choice is at the heart of identifying, creating and maintaining boundaries. When we choose the life we want to lead, we can then create boundaries to provide clarity and enable these choices. Taking time to think about what you *do* want to make up your life in terms of what makes it richer will invariably help you to feel into your agency. In Art 2, *Enough Permission*, we talked about the power of knowing your core purpose and values. This is where they come in handy again. Being present and in touch with your purpose and values allows you to know what you want to say yes to. Your values, as we've already explored, are a profound part of you – they lie deep within your heart.

Take a moment to zoom out of what you have got on your plate right now and give yourself the luxury, just for a few minutes, of standing in the truth of what is most important to you. The trouble with feeling overwhelmed or swamped is that it can skew our perspective and make us feel out of control of what we spend our time on. It can become easy in that state to imagine that your core purpose is something lofty and far away and somehow not quite as important as what you have on your to-do list. Often the reason we don't make choices is not because they are too hard: it is because we forget they are ours to make.

And yet, the truth is that all we have is the present moment. What you do today will either connect to your core purpose and values or it won't. They're not separate – they are entirely connected. When we take a moment to align ourselves to what matters most to us, it connects us back to our agency. Here it is useful to consciously get into your state of Enough Presence. When we are feeling overwhelmed, we are leading with our head. When we remember our purpose and values, we invite our heart back into the conversation, and when we inhabit the present moment, we can listen to our gut brain too. From this deeper perspective, which is connected to our core purpose, working out what matters most becomes easier. Taking it a step further, and allowing yourself to dream for a moment, what is it that makes your soul sing? What is, to borrow a phrase from Gay Hendricks, your 'zone of genius'? That place where you are doing what you do best – in flow – fulfilling your greatest potential; reaching your highest ideal? Asking yourself, 'Am I spending my time doing what I am *good* at, or what I am *great* at?' is a really useful way of prompting your thinking here. We can easily get detached from what we really want to achieve by the busy-ness of our days, so giving yourself the chance to remember this can be very clarifying.

This doesn't have to be separate from your day-to-day life – far from it. You can decide what matters most for each day or each week. A useful way to bring what matters every day into more immediate focus is to think in terms of output and impact, instead of input. Chris Bailey spent a year researching techniques and approaches to being productive in the context of having too much to do. Becoming his own guinea pig, he researched methods and tried them out on himself – making the recommendations in his book, *The Productivity Project*,[4] deeply practical. He found the most useful technique to be one of the simplest. Called the 'rule of three' it is this:

> At the beginning of every day, mentally fast-forward to the end of the day and ask yourself: When the day is over, what three things will I want to have accomplished? Write those three things down. Do the same at the beginning of every week.

Selecting the three most important things to do each day, week or even month or year can of course take a bit of time. If it were obvious, you wouldn't need to focus on it. However, it is a good habit to get into as you commence your days and weeks because although it may take a while to do, the gain is well worth it. David Rock in *Your Brain at Work* explains to us why prioritising is good thing to do at the start of the day or week: 'Prioritizing is one of the brain's most energy-hungry processes.' He goes on to explain: 'It involves understanding new ideas, as well as making decisions, remembering, and inhibiting all at once.' Making choices about which of the many things you need to do first in a day or week might take you half an hour but it's liberating because it can provide such clarity. Rock recommends making it something you do when you feel fresh. Returning to the need to integrate all of your needs, it can be useful to give yourself prompts so that you don't default to only thinking about tasks. For example, 'What will help me learn and grow this week?' or 'What will I do this week to live my values?'

The reason that being explicit and clear in your own mind about the most important, high-impact things each day or week is that there is so much distraction built into each day. Our days are full of multiple demands pulling, pinging, notifying, nagging and competing for our attention, pretty much every minute we are awake. We can be busy from dawn to dusk and still feel as if we have not achieved much. Some days this may feel out of our control. Many of my coaching clients have diaries stacked full of back-to-back meetings that squeeze the available time for the 'rule of three' work into the margins. My challenge to them is that if they are always too busy to do what matters most, then it is time for a significant re-think. Having identified your most important work, you are more likely to be empowered to make more choices about your own diary management –

such as cancelling your attendance at meetings, re-scheduling things so that you have time to focus on your most important output or even to stop some things.

 PRACTICE 12: ENOUGH BOUNDARY #1: WHAT MATTERS MOST

Reflect on these questions:

- What matters most to you?
- How do you decide what this is each year, month, week, day?
- What is most important for your body, your mind, your soul?

Now try whittling down what you have discovered, to one, simple Enough Boundary. Something that you will remember in the heat of the moment – just as the starlings do when they are flying in a murmuration with thousands of other birds. It can be your first 'rule' to keep you on track. Write it down under the heading Enough Boundary #1. As an example, mine for this category is: *Share my learning with others.*

2. UNDERSTANDING YOUR ENERGY PATTERNS

It's one thing knowing what is most important to you; it's another being in the right state to address your most important work when you get to it. We are not machines, and how we feel, how much energy we have, and our ability to switch off other demands in our minds and bodies is critical. How well do you know your own energy patterns? By that I mean, when are you typically most alert in a day and when are you typically more depleted? This isn't of course always the same, but you would be surprised how consistent our physiology can be when it comes to energy. It's a natural rhythm – and we've all got that. You may, for example, be aware of whether you are a 'lark or an owl'. Our diurnal patterns are deeply ingrained. It can be really useful to be more specific about this though. What are the ebbs and flows of your energy throughout the day?

 PRACTICE 13: MAP YOUR ENERGY

Try keeping a log of your energy levels for a week. If you really want to get serious about knowing your natural energy patterns, you can also decide to have a week without stimulants such as caffeine and alcohol.

- Set an alarm for every hour of the day, and simply log a score out of ten for your energy levels at that moment.
- At the end of the week, notice the pattern that has emerged. Write down the timings of your daily high points (sometimes called your 'biological prime time') and when you typically have less energy.

When I did this, I already knew I was an early bird, but this added some detail to that for me – my 'biological prime time' lasts on most days from between 6 and 10am. In addition, I discovered that I am most creative and have my clearest ideas then too. What I didn't know until I collected my own data was that I have another spike of energy between 4 and 7pm most days. Just as predictably, I have lower energy levels for about an hour in the early afternoon – usually between 1 and 2pm after I have eaten lunch. The rest of the day is more evenly balanced in the mid-range. This is such useful data for each of us because it means that we can now predict when we're most likely to be in our best state to do what Cal Newport calls 'deep work'[5]: work that requires intense focus, energy and absorption, which for me is likely to be writing, coaching or designing programmes.

With this data we can start to think in terms of scheduling the opportunity for flow, giving us a sense of meaning, because we are so fully absorbed in what matters most to us. According to Csikszentmihalyi, the psychologist who first described the concept, to achieve flow, three important things need to be in place. Firstly – uninterrupted time, so turn off all notifications. Secondly, the work that you are focusing on needs to be both stretching and absorbing: not intimidatingly hard (which induces a stress response), or too easy (which limits focus and makes us bored and distracted). Thirdly, you need to be in your state of Enough Presence – coherent and in the moment.

Knowing your energy levels is also useful for helping you plan for what Newport calls 'shallow work' – the things that are important and need to be done, but don't require the same level of intensity: emails, for example. Like so many of the people I coach and work with on this, it was revelatory to me to give myself permission *not* to look at my emails first thing in the morning and use up all my most creative 'deep work' energy on that. Now I usually scan them so I can pull out anything that requires deeper levels of focus, and then leave the rest to attend to at one of my mid-energy times.

Equally important is thinking about what you need to do to allow your body and mind to 'rest and digest'. We are not made to always be working at peak intensity – we need times in between to metaphorically exhale. So, knowing what you need to do to take a breather and re-charge your batteries is also important data. For me, the obvious time for this is in my lowest energy time, so when I am able to, I protect the time just after lunch for something that is restorative. Switching off completely or perhaps meditation or a walk.

As always, this is intensely personal. My Art of Enough is unlikely to be yours. Some people working within organizations do not have the same level of autonomy over their time as others. But over time, it's worth looking for even small opportunities to integrate these principles. The more you are able to timetable your days so that you can match what matters most with your energy levels, the more likely you are to experience balance, ease and flow.

 PRACTICE 14: ENOUGH BOUNDARY #2: ENERGY PATTERNS

Reflect on these questions:

- What is your energy pattern?
- Which parts of your work require 'flow'?
- How can you map your work to fit in with your energy pattern?

Again, try whittling down your reflections to create a second, simple Enough Boundary that will help keep you on track for each day. Write it down under the heading Enough Boundary #2.

Mine for this category is the alliterative: *Find flow first thing*.

3. DESIGNING YOUR DAYS, PROTECTING YOUR FOCUS AND SAYING NO

Our third Enough Boundary is for many the most challenging of all, but I believe it is without question the most liberating. By now, you will see that the more you are able to make choices about how you live each day, the more likely you are to remain in the state of Enough, where you have the right amount of energy for the things that matter to you – whatever the level of intensity. In her book, *How to Have a Good Day*,[6] Caroline Webb describes her client Kristen realising that it was on her to create her own boundaries. Kristen says:

> I had this epiphany because I realized that I was mostly mad at me and my lack of boundaries. I'd let things get out of control and I was trying to find someone else to blame. But if I didn't have boundaries, who else was going to give them to me?

Taking control and choosing how you design your life each day can be enormously rewarding. If you are someone who likes a lot of structure, then you may be attracted by Cal Newport's suggestion to: 'schedule every minute of your day'. That's a bit much for me – I prefer to simply timetable my energy to match my output. I block out my higher-energy times in my diary so that I can do activities that require intense focus. As important as timetabling when to do your most important work is when to do your less vital tasks and, of course, when and how to take your breaks.

Designing your days in this way also forces us to think about how interruptible, or not, we choose to be. We live in a world of immediacy – be it the notifications on our devices or the access to world news – and it can be supremely difficult to withstand the temptation to be drawn into needing to know or respond to everything. This is where protecting our focus comes in. Writer Elizabeth Gilbert suggests that we become 'custodians of our own input.'[7] She advocates being a good steward of your mind by curating what your senses are exposed to. Gilbert is not *just* talking about switching off your notifications when you are trying to concentrate on your most important work, although that is of course essential. She's also talking about what and how much you scroll, watch or listen to throughout the day. Thinking of ourselves as a curator of our input can be liberating because, once again, it reminds us that we have choice. Reading our social media or checking the 24-hour news can become highly addictive and habitual, so scheduling time for this can be a useful way of being more intentional.

The same is true whether we are on our own or in a meeting with others. This brings us to multi-tasking. For years, I believed that this was a skill, and that women were especially good at it – by necessity of historically having to juggle several things at once. Sadly, I have come to learn that multi-tasking is a productivity myth. We are simply not capable of doing two things well at the same time. What we do when we think we are multi-tasking is simply do two things less well – and to make matters worse, this takes longer. As Nancy Kline says, 'you cannot multi-task attention'.[8] Microsoft executive Linda Stone coined the term 'continuous partial attention'[9] in 1998, which is what happens when people's focus is split. Stone suggests that when we are surrounded by our digital devices, we are in a state of expecting to be interrupted the whole time, which means that we risk giving only 45% of our attention to anything at any minute. She describes it like this: 'to pay continuous partial attention is to keep a top-level item in focus and constantly scan the periphery in case something more important emerges.' The effect of this? Intense mental exhaustion *and* significantly lower accuracy and productivity. So, creating boundaries and curating when you are available for interruptions will have a significant impact on what you are able to achieve.

Despite this, most of us find ourselves splitting our attention at some point throughout our days, especially because our smartphones make it so easy for us to try. I work with several senior leaders who often look at their phones during meetings. This is because they have a huge volume of emails and very full diaries. It feels like too high a cost to stop responding to emails while they are in meetings, even the most important ones. My challenge to them is always a simple one. If you are reading or responding to emails, you aren't listening with your full attention, which means you are less likely to remember what is said. For something to get lodged in our working memory, it requires focus. If you are not listening during the meeting, it can beg the question: what's the point of you being there? You are giving the signal that the people outside the room are more important than the people inside. This may sound harsh, but it is stacked up by years of scientific research telling us that what's called 'dual task interference' reduces cognitive capacity, meaning that the results of doing two tasks at once are both less accurate and slower. The simple truth is this: it is better to have shorter, more focused meetings and schedule time to do emails afterwards, than trying to do both at the same time. Again, this is an issue that can be met with good, clear scheduling. It's a choice.

Once you have designed your days around the focus you need to give, it's time to really look at how you protect it. This is where I invite you to recruit your inner dragon. Be as robust about your time and focus as you are about anything else you value highly. Get fierce with yourself and others about how important it is. Imagine your inner dragon is sitting on gold, which is your potential to be at your best. In order to protect it rigorously, we need to get really good at stopping things, and saying 'no'.

Over the years of working with busy people, I have observed that the hardest part of holding good boundaries for pretty much everyone is deciding what to stop doing and how to say 'no'. It makes complete, logical sense to stop things, so that we can focus on our most important work. Yet so many people (myself included) behave as if we can still do everything – that we don't have to make any sacrifices in order to focus on what matters most. Choice is all about weighing up cost and gain, and deep down, we all know that we do need to stop things, and if we don't, we risk lowering the standard of everything because we simply don't have the resources to do it all.

 PRACTICE 15: 'STOP DOING' LIST

Business writer Jim Collins in his book, *Good to Great*,[10] recommends creating a 'stop doing list'.

- Write a 'stop doing' list whenever you write your 'to-do' list.
- If you are in a leadership position do this with your team.

- This practice offers such clarity and permission, so role model it, repeat it and make it visible to others.

Identifying what to stop is so often the missing piece of the jigsaw for individuals and teams I work with. Often the most challenging part for them isn't stopping particular tasks, it's stopping the more structural things that feel as if they are 'set in stone' – like the processes or regular meeting patterns. This is entirely the wrong way round but is such a common miscomprehension. When this is the case, I invite people to give themselves permission to create systems and structures that serve what is most important rather than the other way round, so that they are releasing time for themselves and those around them to focus on what matters most. This is so vital to the sustainability of our working life and the success of the organizations we belong to. And there is such freedom in it.

Let's turn to another skill that can enable us to stick to our schedule: saying no to things that we are asked to do. As a serial over-committer, I know how hard this can be – and as a serial over-committer, I have also learned over the years how essential it is to do it well! As one of my early coaches once told me, 'Say no for the bigger yes' and yet another, 'If you never say no it devalues your yes.' Knowing that it is important, though, doesn't stop it feeling toe-curlingly difficult in the moment. We're back to the core Enough concept of cost and gain. It is a case of learning how to tolerate the discomfort in the moment of saying no, so that you can gain the time back for your more important priorities. Brene Brown in *Dare to Lead*[11] invites us to 'choose courage over comfort' in moments that feel difficult to tell the truth. Specifically, from her research she has found that typically the discomfort we feel when we have to speak out in disagreement, give challenging feedback, or in this case say 'no' to something, is eight seconds. Think about that for a moment. You will feel discomfort for eight seconds. You can almost count eight seconds down in your head right after you've spoken up, before the relief of having said no starts to flood in.

There are lots of useful tips about how to say no well. The one I have found particularly useful comes from the Harvard Programme of Negotiations and is sometimes called 'the positive no'.[12] It takes into account what we know about neuroscience and the amygdala's reactions. If we hear a straight, 'No!' to our request, any one of us is highly likely to perceive that as a threat and respond accordingly. The 'positive no' acknowledges our need for psychological safety. I've outlined it below:

- Start with warmth, showing appreciation for the other person's request.
- Explain with genuine enthusiasm what your priority is that will make it unable for you to do the thing you are being invited to do. If possible, this will be something that the other person can understand and empathize with.
- You say no – with regret, you can't do what you've been asked to do.
- You offer, again with warmth, something that you could do which doesn't change the fact that you aren't changing your priorities. For example, if you've been asked to speak at an event, you could offer to recommend someone else that you know would be good.

- Offer good wishes to the person that whatever you are declining goes well.

This process is full of empathy – really standing in the other person's shoes as you speak to them – at the same time as maintaining your own important boundary. It is a helpful process that makes the difficult act of saying no more human, both for you and the person you are turning down.

 PRACTICE 16: KEEP A 'NO' JOURNAL

If you find saying no particularly difficult, or you are in the habit of over-committing, then keeping a 'no' journal can really help. Try recording:

- what you have said no to;
- how you did it;
- how it made you feel in the moment and then again ten minutes later;
- the impact of having said no on your time to focus on what's most important to you;
- what you have done with that time.

Our third Enough Boundary is here to protect and enable us. I believe it is an act of deep self-love and self-respect to learn how to stop doing things. This is true for us as individuals, and it is true for our teams and organizations too. It is underpinned by the clarity that comes when we've reflected on and made good choices.

PRACTICE 17: ENOUGH BOUNDARY #3: PROTECT YOUR TIME AND FOCUS

Reflect on these questions:

- When do you choose to have access to your notifications or switch them off?
- What do you need to stop so that you can focus on the most important things?
- How will you protect your schedule?

Again, the invitation is for you to whittle down your answers to create a third, simple Enough Boundary that, with the other two, will help keep you on track. Write it down under the heading Enough Boundary #3.

Mine for this category is: *Diarize uninterruptable time for 'deep work' each week.*

Once you have identified and written down your three Enough Boundaries, put them where you will see them each day. Committing to them is a question of remembering why they are so valuable to you and forming them into good habits so that they become what you do automatically. This is all very human stuff – some days you may get knocked off kilter, so as always, the trick is to notice, reflect, choose and re-set yourself.

THE JOY OF ENOUGH BOUNDARIES

Let's return to Amani for a moment. When she worked through this process, she discovered small moments where she could make different choices that led to subtle shifts in how she spent each day. Her three Enough Boundaries were:

- timetabled, uninterrupted, quality time with her children at the start, middle and end of the day;
- scheduling an 'actions slot' in the early morning when she had energy, and making herself uninterruptable at that time;
- agreeing with her manager that she would reduce the number of senior management team meetings she attended until her children were back at school.

These didn't stop the demands on her being a lot, but it did stop them feeling overwhelming to her. She re-found her balance – her place of Enough. Amani said this:

> I just feel so much more in control. It's not always easy and I don't always get it right, but I feel as if I am back on track and less torn in two directions at once. Focusing on one thing at a time makes a real difference to me.

These Enough Boundaries were specific to Amani for this particular time in her life – and of course, as our circumstances change, so can our Enough Boundaries so that they stay relevant. The key point is to take the time to reflect and make choices over the things we can control. This will ebb and flow. For some, when the pressure is on, it is only possible to make small adjustments, like Amani. Other times we can make bigger changes. The amount of choice we have depends on our context and what others expect of us. But reflecting, having the conversation with those we are working with, and putting in good boundaries where we can, can have a profound impact on what feels possible.

Just as a murmuration of starlings is enabled to be as magnificent as it is by having three rules, you now have three

Enough Boundaries that will enable you to be magnificent. Good boundaries are containing and enabling. With the help of your Enough Boundaries, you can navigate complexity – like the starlings – with clarity, coherence, ease and agency.

SUMMARY OF *ENOUGH BOUNDARIES*

- Acknowledging the reality of your situation is the first step to being able to make choices about it.
- Boundaries provide clarity, containment and agency.
- In our digital age, you have to set your own boundaries about how you choose to live and work.
- Identify what matters most to you and keep prioritising regularly.
- Get to know your energy patterns and allocate your tasks to fit your energy.
- Protect your time for what matters most.
- Get as good at consciously stopping things as you are at taking things on.
- Give yourself the gift of learning how to say 'no' well.

The transformative potential within Enough Boundaries is…

…finding clarity

119

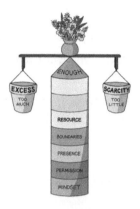

ART 5: ENOUGH RESOURCE

HARNESSING YOUR POWER

That perfect tranquility of life, which is nowhere to
be found but in retreat, a faithful friend
and a good library.

Aphra Behn[1]

*In Art 5, we will explore the resources we need to do Enough.
This can mean internal resource – energy, capability, drive – or
external resource – time, support, others to delegate to. Often
when we are overwhelmed, we can feel disconnected from our*

resources. We will look at Enough Resource as a replenishable cycle and will explore the habits that you can develop in order to sustain yourself in the face of life's demands on you.

Specifically, Art 5 will explore:

- the cyclical nature of Enough Resource;
- the power of mapping what depletes and replenishes you;
- burnout – how to avoid it and build powerful habits to sustain you.

THE CYCLICAL NATURE OF ENOUGH RESOURCE

Often, as a coach listening to what my clients tell me, I could find myself thinking that resources are finite commodities. 'I just don't have the time' or 'I'm running on empty – I'm worn out' or 'I simply don't have the strength anymore.' Sometimes, it's at the opposite end of the finite line – 'There's no stopping me at the moment, I'm like the Dynamo bunny!' or 'I'm always on the go!' While these quotes all express how people feel, they don't quite show us the real picture of how resources work.

I'm wary of people using finite language to describe things that are cyclical and renewable. It's a way of approaching resources that creates anxiety based on a misconception. When we think things will run out, we automatically tip ourselves into a place of Scarcity, which, as we know, triggers our fear-based responses. Neither time, nor strength, nor energy exist in a linear spectrum on a finite line. It's much more accurate and useful to describe them as circular, mirroring the patterns of life and nature that we are familiar with in our everyday lives. Ideally, we get up in the morning, refreshed after a (hopefully) good night's sleep, go through our day meeting the demands, challenges and activities that it holds, have some time to replenish our resources and then return to sleep. Our bodies help us through these cycles of the day, as we explored in the last chapter. Our diurnal pattern is helped by a nervous system and hormones that prime us for action or slow us down to 'rest and digest'.

Thinking of yourself in this circular way can be powerful. Rather than talking about resource as something that will run out and when it's gone it's gone, ask yourself, 'Who or what depletes my energy?' and equally important, 'Who or what replenishes my energy?' It can be useful to compare yourself with something that needs constant replenishment – a phone battery, for example. Our activity uses up the energy in our battery over a period of time, after which we need to plug it in for a while to re-charge. We know this to be true, but some people I work with can be dismissive or even feel a sense of inadequacy about the need to re-charge at all. Given that the quest of this book is to seek ways to find balance – Enough – it is important to remember that our resources are cyclical, with a natural ebb and flow, so that we give time to things that re-charge us at different points throughout any given day, or even a particular season. Probably one of the questions I ask most frequently in my work as a coach is, 'What are you doing at the moment to resource you and re-charge your batteries?' Because it's when we fail to do so that our resilience gets low, and we begin to pay a high cost.

Despite the cyclical nature of our resource patterns, there are of course limits. While natural systems are cyclical, when we overuse them or ignore the need to replenish, they tip out of balance and lose their natural rhythm. They start to unravel and become finite – the circle gets flattened into a line. We see this happening in the world's environment in the 2020s. Having taken too much and pushed it too far, humankind has tipped the planet out of its cyclical patterns towards a linear path of Scarcity. Just as we need to re-balance our use of the world's resources, to restore the natural pattern, the same can be said for each of us. When we routinely ignore our own need to re-charge our batteries over extended periods of time, we too reach a tipping point where we are stretched beyond our natural rhythm. Our resources become linear, and we *do* risk running out of them. In language that mirrors the destructive forest fires in many parts of our climate-challenged world, we risk burning out.

We need to respect the cyclical nature of Enough Resource, whatever that resource is, and to think in terms of setting and re-setting each day. It may be that you already have some regular resilience practices – things that you know resource you and keep you anchored. Yet even those of us who do focus on what can re-charge our batteries can get tipped into Excess or Scarcity by the sheer demands of a day. It's on those days that it helps to remember that we can go back to the start and re-set; that we are able to consciously do something that will give us strength in the face of challenges that seem depleting or overwhelming. For one of my clients, Cynthia, it was deciding, amidst a period of intense pressure for her at work, to sit in her garden for half an hour every lunch time, with no interruptions and the sun on her face. She told me: 'It really works. It's just enough to re-charge my batteries and give me a break from the worries of the day. I really switch off and I come back to my desk feeling rested.'

It's these small, daily practices that can have such positive impact over time. Understanding that a small shift – a conscious re-set – can be Enough is a powerful tool to have at our disposal. We aren't looking for big dramatic gestures that will require us to completely change our lives; we are looking for small regular things to re-balance us back to a place of Enough Resource.

THE POWER OF MAPPING WHAT DEPLETES AND REPLENISHES YOU

 PRACTICE 18: THE WHEEL OF ENOUGH

This exercise can help you to map your life in relation to resource, so that you can identify what to re-set.

- Start by writing a list of all the dimensions of your life that you give energy to. This could be work, family life, creative activity, exercise, voluntary work, time in nature, friendships. Choose your own, as many or as few as feel relevant to you. The aim is to list everything you do that requires your energy. It's important to include things you find life-giving and resourcing as well as things that use up your energy that you have less choice over.
- Draw a wheel, and write one of your dimensions at the end of each spoke. I've used a client's example.

THE WHEEL OF ENOUGH

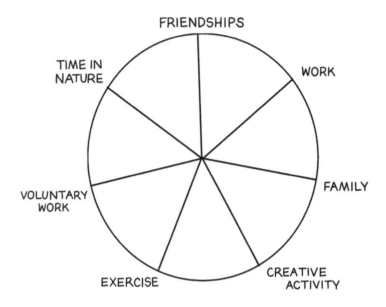

- Give each dimension a score out of ten for how much energy you give it in your daily life. If you find that you don't give much energy to it, it's a low score; a lot of energy gets a high score. Note, this isn't how much you *want* to give each dimension, but the actual amount of energy you currently give it.
- Put a mark on the spoke to indicate your score out of ten, with the inner cog of the wheel representing zero and the outer rim, ten.
- Now connect each of the dots on the wheel with a line. You may end up with something that looks like my client's version.

THE WHEEL OF ENOUGH

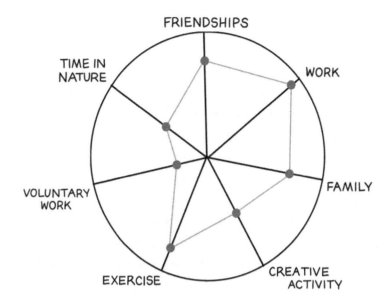

- Look at the pattern of your life and what you give energy to. What do you notice? It's likely that some of the categories might re-charge your batteries, and others deplete them. Reflect on whether you are doing enough to re-charge.
- Now re-visit each dimension and put a mark on the spoke that indicates the amount of energy you would like to intentionally give it.
- Reflect on a small change you could make to balance your energy for each dimension in a more resourcing way. What would make you feel that you have Enough of what you need? Try to avoid any impulse to make everything perfect. One move in the right direction

can have an enormous impact. For example, for one of my clients, it was to finish work at 5pm twice a week to attend an exercise class that she enjoyed; for another, it was starting piano lessons.

- Write down one or two of the small changes that you are prepared to try.

This can be illuminating because it can shine a light on what you are *not* giving yourself by way of resource. So often we focus on the things that we have to do – work or home commitments. And we often miss out the things that may not fall into those categories, but which are intensely rejuvenating. For me it is playing music with friends in a small band that I am part of; it's reading novels; it's going for a run or doing yoga; it's time with close friends. The realization that I had when I did this activity a few years ago was how much I was excluding from my day-to-day life – things that gave me not just energy but joy. I was not giving myself time to do things that feed me, choosing instead to believe that I could not find time for them – or irony of ironies – I was too tired to do them. It is so easy to forget that things that bring joy or energy are actually vital to us finding Enough Resource – they are not luxuries; they are life-givers. When it dawned on me that I was denying myself resourcing activities because I 'didn't have time', I was able to make some small but significant changes to my life and priorities.

INCLUDE EVERYTHING SO YOU CAN INTEGRATE IT

There is more to this than meets the eye. In my work with clients, and indeed reflecting on my own working patterns,

I came to realize that it is not simply about making time for activities that are resourcing; it is about inviting variety and inclusion into how we plan our lives. It is precisely because some of the activities above are so different from my day-to-day commitments that they are so resourcing. The other thing that they have in common is that they are fully absorbing – when I'm playing a song with my band, I can't think about anything else. I'm in flow. I am fully alive to the present moment and not pre-occupied by other concerns be they in the past or future. The power of resourcing yourself by doing something different from your everyday work and family commitments lies in the break it gives you from those very demands. You are being in your body and in the moment in a different way. Doing something that gives your life variety can also offer you confidence and energy from a different source – perhaps one that is more in your control and where the stakes are lower. They are pleasurable in and of themselves. The energy they give you can then carry over to the rest of your life – and as such these activities can provide a powerful contribution to your Enough Resource.

One of the songs we sing in my band is the jazz number 'All of Me'[2] – we sing: *'You took the part that once was my heart. So why not take all of me?'* I think of this song as a plea for wholeness and inclusion and it reminds me of David Whyte's observation: 'You know that the antidote to exhaustion is not necessarily rest? … The antidote to exhaustion is wholeheartedness'.[3] It's important to include everything as you explore what resources you, and that means reflecting on the parts of you that you might not like. Sometimes referred to as your shadow side – it is very easy to ignore the parts of you that you find difficult.

Nevertheless, they *are* part of you, so ignoring them is not including the whole picture. More than that, these aspects of your personality can often be the things that you think will be depleting, but looked at in a different way, they could actually be a resource.

What is your version of 'All of Me'? What could you be leaving out of your resource bank? Think about a counterpoint – not necessarily the opposite – but something that you might naturally exclude when thinking about your resource. Sometimes called the 'path of integration', you are consciously seeking out something different from your natural preference in order to give yourself a counterbalance. This takes some work and commitment, because so often in modern life, we spend our energy avoiding what we don't like or find easy to do. For example, I'm an out-and-out extrovert. I'm energized by being with other people and prioritize the company of others over spending time on my own. More than that, I have a tendency to fear being alone. Over time, I have come to realize that it is precisely because I have to work at enjoying my own company that reflective, introspective time has so much to offer me. This has been a deeply resourcing journey. Time on my own, however hard I find it, balances me and provides me with a sense of wholeness that I was hitherto ignoring. I have learned to like what I once feared; in fact, I sometimes even crave it – something that would have been unheard of ten years ago. As Alan Watts says, 'When you find out that there was never anything in the dark side to be afraid of… nothing is left but to love.'[4] Love is the ultimate resource and the one that holds all others.

PRACTICE 19: INTEGRATING YOUR SHADOW

I've found it useful with coaching clients to find an embodied space for these counterpoint positions. Try this exercise.

- Write down on a piece of paper what you know resources you. In my example, this is 'connecting with other people'.
- Then write down on a different piece of paper the shadow side to that position – something that feels different, but that would provide balance. For me it was 'spending time on my own.'
- Put the two pieces of paper on the floor and move from one to the other, really feeling into each place.
- Imagine that each of these are different parts of you. What would each part say to the other? For example, 'I'm not frightening, I'm part of you too'. Or, 'Sometimes it's exhausting being here the whole time.'
- It can be useful to put down a third marker – to represent your 'wiser self'. When you stand here you can look at the other two positions and observe what each of the positions might offer the other.
- Explore what you could do to find some integration between the two places.

This can be a way to access a deeply balancing resource that you might not have known was available to you – and as such, can be a great addition to feeling that you have Enough Resource.

BURNOUT: HOW TO AVOID IT AND BUILD POWERFUL HABITS TO SUSTAIN YOU

There are few times in a generation that a crisis comes along that affects everyone – and Covid-19 was one. During this time, I worked alongside many individuals and leadership teams; here are some of the things I heard during the long months of the crisis.

'It's been pretty intense. I feel like I'm drinking water from a fire hydrant.'

'I have never experienced such demand – I'm working from 7am until 9pm every day and I haven't had a single day off (including weekends) for weeks.'

'I've cancelled all the holidays I had in the diary. Normally my way of switching off from the high intensity of my work is to take a long weekend every six weeks. I haven't had one for months.'

'I'm so tired that I feel like a tent peg that has been hammered into the earth, and the mallet is still hitting down even though I'm already underground.'

'Everyone is already exhausted and now we face the crisis again. I don't know where we are going to get our energy from.'

These are such profound examples of people under extreme pressure. The combination of the sheer volume of the need to respond to the Covid-19 crisis along with what was, for many, the new experience of working from home, plus an unprecedented sense of urgency making people feel they couldn't stop, meant that many of the people I worked with felt near the point of burnout. The thing they had in common? None of them were able to find time to replenish and re-set their resources. They had reached the end of what, in their state of exhaustion, felt like a finite amount of energy. They felt like they were on a one-way street, giving and giving and giving and not having time to stop, let alone re-charge. The irony is that when we get into this state of exhaustion, we frequently block off the option of asking for help or receiving any support.

I choose to mention Covid-19 in the context of burnout because it is a recognizably familiar crisis that, in diverse ways, affected all of us and pushed us to our limits. It genuinely required some people to work with a level of intensity that felt exhausting. However, there are, of course, many people who work with this level of one-way-street intensity and pressure all the time. There is often a sense of passion, urgency and lack of choice in this state – and it can even be quite stimulating – for a short period of time. But it cannot go on forever.

In order to avoid burnout, it is important to remember the concept of cyclical resource – that we can make choices, however small, to replenish. The rest of the chapter will explore this process in some detail and I'll offer you seven areas of focus that can help you to re-find the power of your Enough Resource. The first three are moving *away* from burnout: they are all about understanding yourself better – exploring your own entanglements and patterns.

The fourth offers you a pivot point – the crucial moment of choice – where you are poised between Excess and Scarcity and can choose to do Enough. The last three offer you ways to move *towards* your Enough Resource so you are empowered by it.

They are:

1. Stop: set a sustainable pace.
2. Avoid giving too much.
3. Understand addictive patterns.
4. Remember you have choices.
5. Learn: think 'post-traumatic growth'.
6. Build your Enough Resource team.
7. Sustain: create habits for Enough Resource.

1. STOP: SET A SUSTAINABLE PACE

Working during a crisis can be incredibly stimulating and provide conditions for work that are deeply motivating. Decision making often becomes quicker and more centralized – therefore less bureaucratic. People can clearly and quickly see the difference they are making. It is often adrenaline fuelled and can feel quite exciting. Teams, even those that do not normally feel particularly aligned, unite together and work towards a shared purpose with clear outcomes. Sometimes teams that are described as dysfunctional can, for the duration of a crisis, come together and work really well. For those with a problem-solving bent, who enjoy action and speed and progress, a crisis can feel highly rewarding – vocational even. A crisis frequently requires long hours, heroic effort, a sense of urgency and everyone pulling in the same direction to work together.

A crisis though, by definition, does not last for ever. The urgency subsides, the need for immediate action and a fast-paced response dwindles. And in our twenty-first-century world, crises are replaced by a 'business as usual' that is more complex and less unified but can still feel challenging, high stakes and relentless. Here decisions, by virtue of being more devolved, take longer to make and there can be a reduced sense of an endpoint. Life outside of a crisis can feel more like painting the infamous Forth Bridge in Scotland – as soon as it's finished on one side, the painters have to start again on the other. But when a crisis ends, the behaviours accompanying it can be harder to stop. We can get stuck in 'crisis gear'. I have worked with many organizations that describe themselves as having a 'hero' or 'crisis as usual' culture. This is because it can feel really energising and fulfilling to work at pace to solve a problem with a sense of urgency. But ultimately working at a crisis pace is exhausting and unsustainable.

There is a definite need, once the first push of a crisis is over, to shift into a more sustainable gear so that individuals and teams are able to manage long-term pressure, volume and complexity. There is a need to consciously move from the driven pace of urgency to one that is more thoughtful and considered. It is after a crisis that we need to re-connect with the clarity of our purpose, vision, meaning and intentional future – we need to stop, reflect, choose, re-set.

Often the first thing that we need after a long period of intense pressure is immediate recovery. Preferably some physical time off but certainly a conscious, psychological break. Next, a re-set – in which we intentionally set a different pace of working. Third, a practical re-design of how we are going to manage the challenges of work for the long term, in a way that is sustainable. This is not about a 'nice to have' or stating good intentions. This is about creating a robust, practical, actionable plan in which individuals and teams think about how to preserve and re-charge energy in order to have the ability to continue to serve their purpose for the long term.

The teams that I have worked with to create a 'sustainable pace plan' have used a range of ideas to give each team member some time off: for example, creating a deputising rota for each other's responsibilities, holding each other to account for taking time off (with no emailing) or sharing support resources. It has proved to be an invaluable way of ensuring that each person takes time away from work – not just relaxing, but consciously doing what it takes for them to re-charge their batteries a bit. It has helped them to be deliberate and disciplined about the need to give themselves Enough Resource – and appreciating the need to do so as one of their key responsibilities.

2. AVOID GIVING TOO MUCH

If you are someone who habitually feels overwhelmed by work, or if you routinely find yourself with too much to do, then it may be worth examining your motivation. What is it that you are feeding when you work too hard? What is the itch you are scratching, the need you are fulfilling? For some I've worked with, it's the culture of their workplace that makes them work long hours – a hero culture where people get rewarded for working 'above and beyond' or 'going the extra mile'. Others can't say no or don't feel that they are allowed to, as we explored in Art 4. Others want to be seen, recognized and appreciated. To quote John Whittington, so often people find themselves 'burning out to belong' – especially if they are working in a culture that encourages and rewards overwork.

Many of us enjoy the feeling of being helpful, of unravelling a problem or making things better. While this is a laudable motivation, it can be the very thing that tips us into overwork – a feeling that we can't stop or that we can never give enough. It can be useful to look at the hidden loyalties or deep patterns in ourselves that are driving us to work in this way. Who in the family or our past is secretly pleased that we're working so hard? So often, we are looking for recognition or approval in the wrong place – we want it from our parents (or someone in our family system), but we're giving all we have to the organization we're in.

When this is the case, I turn again to the work of Bert Hellinger.[5] In his work on uncovering the patterns within all relational systems, Hellinger talks about 'the orders of helping' and offers us some principles that are really useful in looking at what happens in terms of relationship dynamics when we offer help. Hellinger proposes that when we give something to someone, it makes us slightly bigger than them; the more we give, the bigger we become. When you give advice to a friend, client or colleague, you become the person who is right – and you become metaphorically bigger than they are. Think about a time when you, in order to be helpful, gave advice. Does the idea that you become bigger ring true? It does for me, however uncomfortable I find it. To be equal in a relationship – adult to adult – there must be a balance of reciprocity, of exchange. We need to receive as much as we give.

Let's think about this in relation to work. If your purpose is to make things better, in whatever setting you work in, and you spend a lot of your time helping others to solve their problems – whether they are organizational or personal – you are making yourself big in relation to the people you are helping, and this in itself can feel gratifying. Others may become dependent on you. You may become indispensable to them or to the system you are working in. This means that you will be asked to do more and more – it becomes incredibly hard to stop, because the need gets bigger just as you do. You are no longer just helping the system; you have become an integral part of maintaining it, in all its dependency. Many that I have worked with have burnt out doing just this – trapped in the belief that they simply can never do Enough to help.

One way to re-balance this pattern is to look hard at our own motivations to be bigger than other people (sometimes referred to as 'entangled helping'). Hellinger says, 'If we are trying to help someone who does not need our help, then it is we who need the help.' When this is the case, we need to consciously detach from our own desire to help, by stepping away from the issue and leaving the power to decide with the person/team/friend/organization. Seeing things systemically teaches us to be 'useful not helpful'. This distinction is subtle but powerful, because it moves us away from becoming an entangled part of the system. When we understand this, it can free us up to let go of the need to be the one who solves all the problems or makes everything better. We can trust other people and indeed receive what they have to give rather than give it all ourselves. And in doing so, we can save ourselves from burnout.

3. UNDERSTAND ADDICTIVE PATTERNS

Many people I've worked with fall into the habit of overwork, acting as if they are operating in a perpetual crisis. This pattern mirrors that of addiction, and it can be useful to look at it in that way in order to release ourselves from it. Like other addictions, there's a need to look at not just the symptom but the cause. In a pattern that we are becoming familiar with in our exploration of Enough, it is often because we feel an inner sense of Scarcity that we overcompensate with Excess. Dr Gabor Mate, one of the world's most revered thinkers on the psychology of addiction, puts it like this:

> The domain of addiction is where we constantly seek something outside of ourselves to curb an insatiable yearning for relief or fulfilment. The aching emptiness is perpetual because the substance, objects or pursuits we hope will soothe it are not what we really need.[6]

I'm certainly not trying to trivialize or even directly compare severe substance addiction with overwork. Systemically, workaholism can differ from other addictions because it can be so approved of – it can confer status. Yet for me there is a truth and resonance about Mate's words in relation to Enough. It is often the case that people I work with who are in danger of burnout feel unable to stop – they are driven by an insatiable desire to continue. There is something about what the work is giving them that feels essential, and stopping can feel scary because it can force them to look at what they might be 'too busy' to attend to.

If this is the case for you, think about what it is you are gaining by being perpetually in the domain of Excess. What would it cost you to stop overwork or busy-ness? It may be that it is covering up something that is more difficult for you to look at. It requires a leap of faith and a lot of courage to move away from something that is exhausting but familiar to look at something that may actually feel more painful. In my experience, though, it is always a leap worth taking because it can lead you back to a place of balance – where you feel that you *are* Enough and so you can *do* Enough, not too much.

4. REMEMBER YOU HAVE CHOICES

Over the years, I have noticed that one of the symptoms of someone on the road to burnout is that they perceive themselves as having no choice but to do what they are doing. It can feel impossible to stop and look at the whole – to see the proverbial wood from the trees. And yet it is essential. This is the pivot point in finding Enough Resource to avoid burnout. We are seeking the delicate balance of Enough. We always have the choice to become present; and we always have the choice to move from a focus on the problem to a focus on the solution.

 PRACTICE 20: WORKING PATTERN REVIEW

How often do you step back and review your working pattern? This is a vital ingredient to helping you to move away from the Excess bucket and into Enough, which is more sustainable.

- You know that each day requires you to use energy and to renew your energy. Frame your work design with the requirement to include something that re-charges you.
- Re-visit the question: what is it that you can intentionally build into each day or each week that re-charges your batteries? Whatever it is – choose to build it in. It matters. Whether it relates to exercise, sleep, rest, time away from work, variety/fun activities outside of work is entirely up to you.

- Imagine your ideal working pattern. Write it down. How many hours a day or week would you be working? Think back to your 'Wheel of Enough'. Identify what is within your personal control. What choices are available to you? What can you change so that you are doing Enough?

The key is that in making a choice, you give yourself power and agency – from a position of self-compassion. You move from blindly following patterns and habits to consciously deciding what patterns and habits you want to create for the life you want to live. So many of us spend our time focusing on the problem in front of us instead of finding a solution. The adage 'energy flows where focus goes' is a great reminder that we have most power when we give our attention to what we want to achieve rather than what we want to avoid. When we commit our Enough Resource wholeheartedly to moving beyond the problem to the solution, we are filling ourselves with our own power.

5. LEARN: THINK 'POST-TRAUMATIC GROWTH'

I've always found Nietzsche's phrase 'what does not kill me makes me stronger' a bit trite – comparing difficult situations to the very worst outcome usually feels reductive and irrelevant when I'm at a low ebb. However, there is a truth in the fact that pretty much every human experience – however painful – contains some learning. In their book *Option B*,[7] Sheryl Sandberg and Adam Grant describe ways that Sandberg found to cope after the sudden and unexpected death of her husband, with the help of her friend – psychologist Grant.

One of the things they describe is how much it can help to think not just in terms of bouncing back from difficulties but bouncing forwards – learning from what has happened.

This isn't particularly new – David Kolb's experiential reflective practice learning cycle[8] (a staple for adult educationalists and learners alike for decades) suggests that the best learning often comes from reflecting on experiences, drawing conclusions and then applying what you have learned to the next time you do it. However, having worked in this space for over 20 years, I have lost count of how many times I ask people in organizations how they reflect and learn from what they do, only to hear the familiar response: 'We hardly ever do – and only if something goes wrong.' So, the idea of reflecting and learning from adversity in order to build resilience is a great idea and one that we still need to remember to build into our lives.

Psychologists Richard Tedeschi and Lawrence Calhoun[9] in their research into people recovering from trauma and grief go one step further. They coined the term 'post-traumatic growth'. This is particularly helpful as it acknowledges the fact that something has been traumatic, at the same time as offering people a way of thinking about how to frame their recovery. The key to relating this to Enough Resource and finding balance as opposed to burnout is, of course, time to reflect. As a coach, nearly everyone I work with is time poor. All of my clients have demanding roles, lots of responsibility and work in the context of high levels of complexity. What coaching offers them, even for a couple of hours a month, is time out to reflect, draw conclusions about what they have done and learn from them. Whether you have a coach or not, taking time out to reflect on what learning you can draw from a difficult, even traumatic, event or season is invaluable. A period of sense-making can help you to understand what happened, reflect on what was resourcing and depleting in the moments that mattered, and ask yourself the question, 'Where is the growth in this for me/us?'

Having said that, I appreciate that it can feel like an oxymoron to suggest to someone nearing a state of burnout to take time out to reflect. And I am fully aware that asking someone, 'What are you learning?' mid-crisis may very well not be wise – I know it would irritate me! Timing is everything, and most people will need a little space to process before they can find learning from a situation. Nonetheless, reflection, taking time to pause and notice can be deeply resourcing. And it is not necessarily just a thought process – we get a lot of data from our bodies, and they often send us early warning signals and remind us of the need to re-balance. When we remember to ask our bodies, 'What are you trying to tell me?', especially if we are tired or feeling run down, we include crucial data for what we need. We can then start to find the meaning and learning so that we can integrate it into our lives.

6. BUILD YOUR ENOUGH RESOURCE TEAM

Having a good team around you can make all the difference when looking at how you create Enough Resource for yourself. There are two ways of looking at team from this perspective: firstly, thinking about external resource, having a team of good people to delegate to at work. Secondly, looking internally, having a team of personal champions who resource you to be your best.

Firstly, let's look at having a good team to delegate to. At risk of stating the obvious, when thinking about Enough Resource in the context of Excess, overwhelm and volume of work, being surrounded by really good people and delegating successfully to them is vital. Not everyone has a team or teams to delegate to – in which case you can skip to point 2. If you do, there is plenty of fantastic literature dedicated to how to do this well, so I'm offering highlights with a couple of examples here. In essence, the research points to four key areas:

- **Have the right people in your team(s)**: In *Good to Great*, Jim Collins makes the convincing case for having 'the right people on the bus, in the right seats and the wrong people off the bus'.

- **Don't be shy about equipping yourself with the resource you need to do your job effectively**: In her research into *Senior Leadership Teams*,[10] Ruth Wageman suggests that once you have the right team of committed and highly competent people in place in your team, the next step is to give them a good level of resource. Her research finds that: 'The leaders of great teams don't assume that it is an insult to the ingenuity and expertise of the members to make sure that they have access to all the resources they need to carry out their work at the highest levels of excellence.' This goes both ways of course. It's important to check that the people being delegated to are well-resourced themselves. Everyone, at every level within an organization, needs to be well-resourced and supported, and the organizations that understand this well are the healthiest and usually the most productive too.

- **Build a culture of trust and autonomy:** Kouzes and Posner in their 30-year-long rolling research into *The Leadership Challenge*[11] offer some great tips for creating the right climate in a team for good delegation to happen, where people feel empowered, trusted and able to make decisions, with appropriate levels of support and guidance. Key here is that delegation is *not* just dumping on others; it's supporting them to do it well. As team dynamic aficionado, Patrick Lencioni[12] suggests, for a team to be functional, it needs to be built on a firm foundation of trust. This allows all members of the team to trust others to make decisions, do what needs to be done, set up open lines of communication for updates or an open conversation at any point if things aren't going to plan, on time or if there's an issue with the standard of delivery.

- **Clear roles and clear accountability:** I have worked with so many teams where the person who is delegating becomes the bottleneck for signing work off because they have not delegated responsibility for quality control or decision making. One team I worked with had 11 people checking a report between the person writing it and the person leading the team, which meant that, in reality, no one was taking responsibility for the standard of the work – everyone thought that someone else in the chain would be making the corrections. Clarity about who is doing something, who else needs to be involved, the standard to which it needs to be done and who is signing it off, needs to be in place at the outset. When it is, delegation works well and everyone, wherever they are in the chain of delegation (yourself included), has Enough Resource to ensure a great outcome.

Secondly, let's explore how resourcing it is to have a team of champions. I work with a lot of people who have senior strategic roles but don't have a team – they need to work horizontally across their organizations to influence a range of different stakeholders. I have also coached many people who don't work with a team of direct reports for other reasons. Whatever *your* circumstances, we all need a team of champions. These are the people who have got our backs, who cheer us on and who enable us to do what is required of us, even when that is challenging.

Sometimes this can come in the guise of a specific work mentor – someone who has been doing what you do for longer and is prepared to offer a guiding hand, a space to talk about work and to offer support and encouragement. I always think of mentors like relay runners: at the start of our careers, if we're lucky, we receive guidance from a mentor, and then as we progress, we start to offer our own mentoring to others coming behind – a chain of wisdom being passed down the line. In addition to a mentor, I encourage all my clients to find their allies or champions in their organizations and their network – not just to help them to thrive in their roles to be the best they can be, but so that they have someone to turn to for resource when things are tough. On days when you are feeling not Enough, whether that is due to Scarcity or Excess, it is often these people who are going to help you re-balance.

Knowing that you have these people on your Enough Resource team is already really powerful. There will be times when all you need to do is to bring them to mind, and this will give you the resource you need. I often invite my coaching clients to think of each person who resources them – in and out of work, from their past or present – and write each name on a different post-it note. They put the notes behind them and stand, facing whatever the challenge they have ahead of them, with their resources literally at their back.

You can go further and select a couple of people from your 'Enough Resource team', write their names on a piece of paper and put them in your pockets for when you are doing something that you may need extra support for. I've done this for talks and meetings that I've been nervous about and have found it really great to feel my resource team literally in my back pocket when I need them most. The people you draw on can change, depending on what you need resourcing for. You may select someone who you know does what you do particularly well. You may choose someone who cares deeply about you being the best you can be and always roots for you. Or you may even choose a client that you have done a great piece of work with. Whatever it is, the aim is to find someone who consciously supports you and will fill you with a sense that you are fully resourced to be Enough in the moments that matter.

7. SUSTAIN: CREATE POWERFUL HABITS TO SUSTAIN YOU

In her wonderful book about writing, Anne Lamott[13] tells this story – a great strategy in the face of overwhelm.

> Thirty years ago my older brother, who was ten years old at the time, was trying to get a report on birds

written that he'd had three months to write. It was due in the next day... he was at the kitchen table close to tears, surrounded by binder paper and unopened books on birds, immobilized by the hugeness of the task ahead. Then my father sat down beside him, put his arm around my brother's shoulder and said, 'Bird by bird, buddy. Just take it bird by bird'.

Habits are notoriously hard to change, especially behavioural habits – things that we always do. Most people will share the experience of trying to start or stop something, and it proving to be too difficult to maintain over time. Look at the statistics of gym memberships, which routinely spike in January along with our New Year's resolutions and then dip again by March. So, in order for you to change what you do each day, to ensure that you have Enough Resource for the challenges you routinely face, it takes practice and intention.

As we've already explored, it is useful to start small. Set yourself achievable changes, rather than big, life-changing gestures. I actually don't know anyone who really has made the fantasy life-altering change that are sometimes reported in lifestyle magazines – you know the ones, where people give up the rat race to live self-sufficiently on a beautiful smallholding somewhere. But I do know and have worked with literally hundreds of people who have made small adjustments to how they live and work, which have had a huge impact on their lives. Sir David Brailsford, the head of British cycling for years, famously came up with a programme of what he called 'marginal gains', where he looked at every single thing that contributed to a successful Olympic cycling race and sought to make a small improvement to each one. He said of this approach, 'If you break down a big goal into small parts, and then improve on each of them, you will deliver a huge increase when you put them all together.'[14] His success in doing so is well documented; the British cycling team went from one Olympic gold medal to eight in as many years. And so it can be for you. If you want to live a more balanced life where you are powered by your resources in a state of Enough, then the changes that you make don't have to be huge. What they need to be is consistent. As Anne Lamott's father said, 'bird by bird'.

In *Atomic Habits*,[15] James Clear explains the psychology of how habits work, and the things that we do that will make habits stick. One of his insights that is particularly helpful is where we focus when we decide to change our behaviour.

- Firstly, we can focus on the *goal or outcome* of what we want to change – this is the result of the change. For example, a more sustainable work pace.
- Secondly, we can focus on the *processes* – what we do to effect the change. For example, Cynthia from earlier in the chapter taking half an hour in her garden every lunch time in order to re-charge her batteries.
- Thirdly, we can focus on our *identity* – our self-image, what we believe about ourselves. For example, for you it could be: 'I am Enough, I do Enough and I have Enough.' When we focus on the belief behind our behaviour, we are much more likely to stick to the long-term changes we make. As Clear says, 'Improvements are only temporary until they become part of who you are. The goal is not to read the book, the goal is to become a reader. The goal is not to run a marathon, the goal is to become a runner.' For us, the goal is to live well with the Art of Enough.

When it comes to selecting and sticking to regular practices that give you Enough Resource, it can help to draw on those people you have recruited to be in your resource team. Accountability partners can make a huge difference to making behaviour change habits stick – whether they are part of your formal support, such as your line manager, peer group, or coach – or whether they are a close friend or family member. Once you have decided what it is you want to become, articulate it to someone who matters to you, and recruit them to be your support.

THE POWER OF ENOUGH RESOURCE

Finding Enough Resource is always going to be work in progress – our lives are full of complex demands both in and out of work. Finding a pattern of living which consciously gives you the ability to feel that you have Enough Resource is a crucial ingredient to you finding your own Art of Enough. When you make choices, learn from your experiences, remember who is on your team and create habits that will keep you on track: you are stepping into the power that all of us have within us to actively resource what it is that we want to do in the world.

SUMMARY OF *ENOUGH RESOURCE*

- Your resources are cyclical.
- Get to know what depletes and replenishes you.
- Create a rhythm of replenishing your resources regularly, in and out of work.
- Include everything – integrate all of you.

- Variety can be energising.
- It is often our entanglements that drive us to burn out – have a look at your pace, your motivation to help and your addictive patterns.
- Choose to be resourced.
- Power yourself by your learning, your 'team' and your habits.

The transformative potential within Enough Resource is…

…harnessing our power

PART 3

THE ART OF *HAVING* ENOUGH

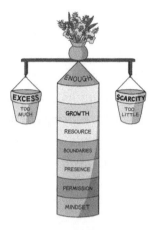

ART 6: ENOUGH GROWTH

THE WISDOM OF GROWING SUSTAINABLY

There is enough, enough for all
And much besides to spare
Yet hundreds daily, hourly fall
From want and woe and care.

The earth would be a holy place
As paradise above
Could we but teach the human race
Equality and love.

From 'Poor Man's Lamentation', 19th-century ballad by Uriah Smart[1]

In Art 6, we will explore the freedom of limits. As a society we massively overconsume and throw away more each year than our forebears ever had in a lifetime. These behaviours have brought us to the brink of environmental collapse and have not made us happier either. Even the concept of Enough Growth can feel limiting or restrictive to some. For others, it can be a byword for mediocrity and a lack of ambition. Here we are going to turn that thinking on its head and explore Enough Growth as the doorway to realising our ambitions, fulfilling our maximum potential and finding happiness. We'll look at how we can achieve Enough Growth – individually and collectively – so that we can flourish and thrive without it costing the earth.

We will explore:

- *the Enough Growth cycle;*
- *the freedom of limits;*
- *the myth of never-ending growth;*
- *doughnut thinking;*
- *when less is more;*
- *dreams of transformation.*

THE ENOUGH GROWTH CYCLE

As a young child, one of my favourite books was *The Very Hungry Caterpillar* by Eric Carle.[2] It gave me such pleasure seeing the holes in the board book increase as the picture of the caterpillar moved through the pages. The illustrations follow the journey of a caterpillar grub, who becomes hungrier and hungrier as he munches through his food with insatiable appetite. The more he eats, the more he wants to eat. There is no stopping him… until of course eventually the time comes for him to form into a chrysalis. It turns out, as we know, that growing bigger isn't the end game for him; it's transformation – becoming a butterfly. But of course, the caterpillar doesn't know that – until he lives it. There is an obvious metaphor here for the world we currently live in. We consume and consume and consume, ever hungry, never sated, until we realize that endless consumption isn't the point. It's not what makes us happy or fulfilled – transformation is.

The metaphor of metamorphosis is a useful frame for us as we consider Enough Growth. How we think about growth matters because our collective focus on growth at the expense of anything else has brought our planet to the brink of what is known as the 'sixth mass extinction'. We are at a tipping point of global eco-system change as a result of our focus on producing more, whatever the cost. However, despite the messages we receive from neo-liberal economists, governments and the media, growth is not always only about getting bigger; it's about depth, learning, imagination, creativity and transformation. And, as we've explored already, like the caterpillar's imaginal cells, we all carry the potential not just for getting bigger but for realising unexpected transformation and beauty within us.

Borrowing from the world of biomimicry, I have created a new model for us to think about Enough Growth – which draws its inspiration from the natural world. As you would expect, it is cyclical not linear. In following nature's pattern, we can explore how to escape the see-saw of Scarcity and Excess to find our balance point of Enough from which we can flourish and grow. Metamorphosis is of course not the only way that growth happens in the natural world. Most things do not entirely change form as part of their growth – rather, once they reach their 'right size', they focus their energy on becoming fully themselves. I have nevertheless included transformation as a fourth stage because to exclude the allure and magic of the 'imaginal cells' (as we discussed in the Introduction) seems to me to miss out some of the inherent potential within us all.

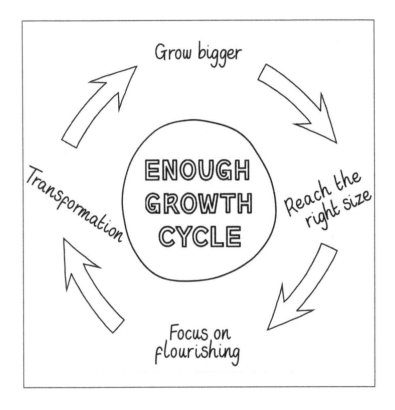

Stage 1: grow bigger. From babyhood to adult, from fledgling idea to something fully formed. This is the stage where we are hungry to learn, to grow, to develop. It is the stage of higher consumption and fast growth.

Stage 2: reach the right size. We stop growing outwardly. We reach our right size and settle into it – our natural, physical limit.

Stage 3: focus on flourishing. We focus our energy and resources on reaching our potential – on living a full existence; thriving within the natural boundaries that keep us contained and healthy.

Stage 4: transformation. As we learn from the caterpillar, transformation requires letting go of the old state to make room for the new one. A bit of us has to die, perhaps old identities or laying the ego to rest. We need to let go of what was, in order to become something new – something quite different, astonishing and beautiful, sourced from our imaginal cells.

The challenge we have at the moment is that much of our culture and society are stuck in Stage 1 – where we are focused only on growing bigger – as if the other stages do not exist. The balance of exchange is wrong; we take too much and fail to give back to the earth or replenish the resources. All in the name of growth. Not only have we rejected the idea of limits, we've forgotten how essential they are in enabling us to move on to the next stages, where we can shift our focus and effort onto flourishing, thriving and realising our dreams of transformation. We need to allow ourselves to move on from insatiable consumption so that we can find a way for us all to flourish in partnership with the rest of the planet.

It's easy when talking about the larger systemic picture and what has got us here for us to feel judged for the way we live, or indeed judgemental of ourselves and others. It is easy to critique and fall into a binary of right and wrong. As a counter to that, I offer this chapter in the spirit of curiosity and exploration of the wider context we live in. It is a genuinely heartfelt enquiry into how we can, individually and collectively, find a way to think about Enough Growth that has a positive impact on the planet we share.

For me, the quest for Enough Growth is resourced by my feelings as well as my rationality – it's about love and heartbreak and hope. Have you ever felt your heart lift when you hear a bird sing first thing in the morning, or gasped as you looked up at the multitude of stars at night? Has the sight of a sunset made you want to weep with the beauty of it? Or, like me, have you stopped and marvelled with a thrill of hope at the simple beauty of a crocus in an urban park in February signalling the coming of spring? And then, have you ever felt heartbreak at seeing litter bobbing in the eddies of a river or strewn across a beautiful beach? Or cried at the end of watching a nature programme where you have been consumed by the beauty of our world, only to see how the habitats are being destroyed the world over? (Like many I'm sure, I've been known to sob at the end of a David Attenborough documentary.) And have you ever shared with me a deep sense of longing that we can reverse the crisis that we stand on the cusp of now, and find ways to live which, far from costing the earth, replenish it? In my experience, when we allow ourselves to really engage with our emotions as well as our minds, we fill ourselves with a sense of agency and action. We are more compelled to act because we have experienced our reactions wholeheartedly.

Far from being entirely sad and hopeless, I believe that rising to this challenge could just be the most joyful one of our lives. Learning how to live with Enough Growth is learning how to include all stages of growth – and this calls for us to draw on the best of ourselves – love, courage, hope and creativity. I believe that this will lead us to new ways of flourishing: living with the Art of Enough is in itself something to aim for because it gives us so much, both inwardly and outwardly. It is both intensely personal and immensely social. We each need to find our way to what makes us flourish and then come together to share in that process.

In this chapter, we'll explore the full cycle of growth; how we can find a balance of Enough by living with conscious awareness of Stages 2, 3 and 4 – working on the assumption that we are already really good at Stage 1. We'll look at Enough Growth with an individual lens and a systemic one – and explore how what we do mirrors the wider environment. Here we are looking at growth as the opportunity to draw on what we have learned about how to *be* and *do* Enough and build on this state of balance so that we can *have* Enough of what we need in order to thrive – to really reach our potential. We'll start by unpacking perhaps the most challenging yet ultimately liberating stage of Enough Growth: knowing what our limits are and learning how to stop.

REACH THE RIGHT SIZE: THE FREEDOM OF LIMITS

Even talking about limits can be a challenge. We are so immersed in the culture of exponential growth being good that contemplating the idea of limitations on us can feel, well, restrictive, and I for one don't like the idea of being constrained. It seems to be the antithesis of freedom. And yet limits exist whether we like talking about them or not. We all stop growing taller when we reach adulthood. Everything in nature stops growing bigger at some point

– it has its own in-built limit. Whether it is a fish, reptile, mammal or tree, it stops growing. It is perhaps more useful, then, to think of limits not as something negative that stop us, but as something positive – containers that enable us and keep us safe. Limits, like the Enough Boundaries we explored in Art 4, help us to stop when we need to so that we can focus our energy and attention on other things. And knowing when to stop growing bigger doesn't have to limit our sense of possibility; in fact, the opposite is true – it can release it. When we say, 'the sky's the limit', what we are calling on is our ability to transform. As business writer Charles Handy writes in *The Second Curve: Thoughts on Re-inventing Society*,[3] 'If we cannot ever say to ourselves, "enough is enough" we will never be free to explore other possibilities.'

Let me give you an example of what this might mean in practice. I was lucky enough to meet with Charles Handy and his wife Liz when I was in the early stages of developing this book, and they told me how they both managed the cycle of their working lives by setting themselves limits. As Charles told me:

> Now at the start of the year, we decide how much money we need to earn for the year ahead. We put a limit on it, and we only accept work that takes us to that limit. When we have already been booked for projects that reach our upper financial limit, we turn our attention to things that we do that do not give us money. They give us other things.

The wonderful twinkle in Charles's eyes as he said this spoke volumes to me about how valuable this was for them.

As someone who has worked for myself for the majority of my working life, I found this idea both liberating and challenging. What would it really be like to turn down work once I'd hit the amount I needed to earn to meet my financial needs? Of course, this is not a choice that is available to everyone. Many people work hard in full-time work and still struggle to earn enough to get by, and for them, a limit on income is the opposite of liberating. (We will discuss the importance of a fair and distributive economy later in the chapter.) Nevertheless, for me as someone who had spent the previous few years working as hard as I could, earning as much as I could (for a 'rainy day'), the idea of setting myself a maximum income target as well as a minimum income target from a business perspective was a new one on me, and gave me pause for thought. It made me realize how much I had adopted the behaviours and practices prevalent in our society which tell us that more is always better – that there is no end point when it comes to revenue and, indeed, financial growth. When I finally had the courage to give myself permission to do this (drawing on some of the activities in Art 2, *Enough Permission*), I found it to be a massive relief. Blocking out time and turning down work certainly turned my working practice on its head, and it genuinely released me to do other things that resource me and help me to flourish in other ways, to focus on other parts of my life that are important and that had been at times neglected. In setting my own limit to growth, I felt free. It turns out that limits didn't stop my growth: they were a prerequisite for it.

As Charles Handy pointed out to me, there are plenty of examples of businesses that do this. Much of the German economy is made up of family-owned manufacturing businesses, which are not listed on the stock market. It is essential for these businesses to continue to be innovative and top quality, and without the short-termism of shareholder growth directing their attention to immediate profits, they are able to re-invest back into their business. I once coached a senior director in Bosch – the globally successful and still family-owned business – who told me with great pride that 97% of their annual profits were fed back into the business, and that their strategic forecasting went 30 years into the future. The limit to the amount of profit they take out of the business frees them to invest it in their people, in research, innovation and quality. Sustainability is more important for them than short-term gain.

There are also many examples of businesses that choose to grow to the 'right size' and no bigger. I'll tell you the story of one I know well. For 15 years, I was one of the directors of an independent fostering agency, whose visionary founder and CEO, Janet Digby-Baker, insisted that we never grew beyond a certain size. Janet would tell us all regularly that in order to maintain a personal relationship with all the 'looked after children' and the foster carers on our books, we had to stay relatively small – or more accurately – the right size. This meant that the agency was able to focus on the values and standards of care that Janet was so passionate about. For instance, every child was given a bike and taught how to swim, so that they could develop life skills which, in her decades of work as a social worker and in the family law courts, Janet had noticed were often overlooked for children in care. Staying small enough – the right size – was the key to enabling the company to live its values driven by its purpose and focus relentlessly on the quality of care given to vulnerable children. Of course, this took commitment and discipline; as a result of the focus on quality, the agency was popular, and it would have been easy to exceed the self-imposed limit and grow bigger. But we never did – and I learned first-hand how rewarding and impactful this decision was.

REACH THE RIGHT SIZE: THE MYTH OF NEVER-ENDING GROWTH

Why is it that the myth of never-ending growth has been so compelling to us, despite the fact that is obviously so flawed? In part, I think it is because it chimes so well with something deeply personal and individual for all of us: the idea of a constant striving to belong. In his famous novel, *The Great Gatsby*,[4] F. Scott Fitzgerald beautifully encapsulates the sense of material wealth replacing a sense of belonging for the characters. The novel ends with these poetic words:

> Gatsby believed in the green light. The orgastic future that year by year recedes before us. It eluded us then, but that's no matter – tomorrow we will run faster, stretch out our arms farther… And one fine morning — So we beat on, boats against the current, borne back ceaselessly into the past.

It is in the constant craving for the elusive tomorrow that we are seduced into wanting more and never being satisfied with what we have. And as Fitzgerald suggests, this requires us to look back into our own systems. This collective cultural longing calls on each of us to look 'into the past' of our own lives and ask, 'Who am I being loyal to?', 'Who am I doing this for?', or 'What pain am I running away from or craving to heal?' As Fitzgerald's famous novel helps us realize (and as we have explored earlier in this book), it is only when we attend to our own longing – and belonging – that we can be free of the allure of wanting more.

This chimes with the definition of addiction that we explored in the last chapter. Returning to Gabor Mate's work, he describes asking the addicts he works with what they gain from the particular substances they take:

> I ask them, 'What in the short term, did it give you that you craved or liked so much?' And universally, the answers are, 'It helped me escape emotional pain; helped me deal with stress; gave me peace of mind, a sense of connection with others, a sense of control.'[5]

In so many ways, this strikes me as similar in motivation to our societal habits of consumption. How many of us talk about 'retail therapy', or use shopping and material gain to make us feel somehow better, more in control, less stressed or even to sooth our pain? I know that I have bought things that I don't need, be they clothes or food or experiences, to do all of the above. Which is why I believe that Enough Growth is intrinsically linked to all of the other aspects of Enough that we have explored in this book – our inner sense of who we are. How we feel about ourselves impacts on how overstretched we become in our lives and work, which in turn impacts on how we consume. When we have Enough Presence – feel that we *are* enough and can *be* fully in the present moment, then we can make the choices that free us up to *do* Enough and we start being conscious of what it is we need in order to *have* Enough. And in finding our state of Enough, we can thrive.

Widening our lens a little, another reason that we can overlook seeing the freedom inherent in limits is that at a macro level for the last century neo-liberal economics has told us that growth, as in 'more and bigger', is the most important thing for us to focus on. A country's economy is measured by the rate of growth of its GDP (Gross Domestic Product). This is despite the fact that many economists, politicians, philosophers and environmentalists have argued for decades that using only GDP as a measure of economic success is at best incomplete, and at worst, destructive. An increasing number of economists, from E.F. Schumacher in his seminal text, *Small is Beautiful*[6] in 1973 and more recently Kate Raworth in *Doughnut Economics*,[7] present the full picture as to why this is damaging. By only measuring what the collective endeavours of a nation makes, we omit to count the cost.

Systems thinker, Donella Meadows, one of the co-authors of a UN-funded report in 1972 called *Limits to Growth*,[8] put it bluntly in a talk she gave in 1999:

> Growth is one of the stupidest purposes ever invented by any culture. We've got to have enough… we should always ask, 'growth of what, and why and for whom, and who pays the cost, and how long can it last, and what's the cost to the planet, and how much is enough?'[9]

Despite persistent warnings from a host of learned people, we are only beginning to really understand the extent of the damage that our addiction to growth has caused to the global climate and eco-system, and indeed to the distribution of wealth across the globe.

It would seem that we've been conditioned into believing in the idea that we can continue to grow and that nothing will run out. In *The Story of Stuff,*[10] an animated short film, and subsequently a book of the same name, Annie Leonard talks us through the cycle of consumerism. Sometimes known as the 'take, make, use, lose' economic cycle, Leonard explains that the consumerist system was deliberately designed in post-war America as a way to re-boot the economy. Since then, industrial countries the world over have been following the cycle of extracting resources from the earth, manufacturing them into products with a short lifespan (cynically called 'designed obsolescence'), and selling them to us consumers who will end up throwing them away because they either break or go out of fashion or both. As economist Tim Jackson put it in his 2010 TED Talk, 'We are persuaded to spend money we don't have on things we don't need to make impressions that won't last on people we don't care about.'[11] This is, of course a linear system and one that pretends that the world's resources are endless. As we explored in Art 5, that isn't how nature works. Without time to replenish, resources *do* become finite. This consumerist system has an inevitable end point, one in which the world's resources run out. As it turns out, Gandhi was right when he said, 'Our earth provides enough to satisfy everyone's need, but not for everyone's greed.'[12] And perhaps even Gandhi didn't anticipate how hard we would find it to stop.

How can we find Enough Growth against this personal, economic and cultural backdrop? Well, at a macro level, we can start by including a wider spectrum of measures. Using only GDP as the measure of economic success is flawed because it is so one-dimensional. By only looking at one small part of the picture, we allow ourselves to believe the impossible – that growth has no limit. As long ago as 1968, Robert Kennedy said:

> GDP measures neither our wit nor our courage, neither our wisdom nor our learning, neither our compassion nor our devotion to our country: it measures everything in short except that which makes life worthwhile.[13]

So for us to seek the balance of Enough Growth, we need to include more data, measure more parts of the equation, include a more holistic picture of ourselves as humans and of the world and its resources. This is where *Doughnut Economics* come into play.

FOCUS ON FLOURISHING: DOUGHNUT THINKING

Having explored the freedom that limits to growth can give us, let's delve into the next stage in the growth cycle, flourishing, and how we can continue to grow in different ways. Economist Kate Raworth[14] called her economic model the 'doughnut' because it has clearly delineated inner and outer limits to the economy – not dissimilar to the ones we've already described for ourselves earlier in this chapter. Raworth offers this way of seeing the economy as a way of creating, 'A world in which every person can lead their life with dignity, opportunity and community – and where we can all do so within the means of our life-giving planet.'[15]

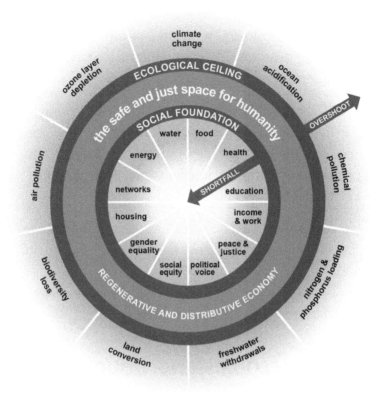

On the inside of the doughnut is the boundary of 'social foundation' – the *minimum* that every human in the world needs in order to live a life of dignity. Driven by a desire for social justice and a distributive economy, this boundary contains 'food, water, energy, networks, housing, gender equality, social equity, political voice, peace and justice, income and work, education and health'. If any of these categories are not met by all people, then we are operating in the realm of what Raworth calls 'shortfall' – akin to what we're describing as Scarcity.

The outer boundary of the doughnut is 'ecological ceiling' – the *maximum* limit that we need to live within to keep our planet healthy. This is made up of 'climate change, ozone layer depletion, air pollution, biodiversity loss, land conservation, freshwater withdrawals, nitrogen and phosphorus loading, chemical pollution, and ocean acidification'. When we go beyond the planetary boundary on the outer edge of the doughnut, we are in the realm of 'overshoot' – what we're calling Excess.

Within these two limits is the doughnut itself, the domain of thriving – what Raworth calls, 'The safe and just space for humanity' underpinned by a 'regenerative and distributive economy'. We're calling it Enough. For the world to thrive, all of humanity (not just the chosen few) needs to thrive and vice versa, and when we live within the boundaries described, we can focus on how we live well. We can focus our energy on flourishing – the third stage of our Enough Growth cycle. Raworth presents a powerful and comprehensive description of ways in which our economy can transform so that both humanity and the planet can thrive. What we need to do is, of course, learn how everyone can live full and rich lives within these limits.

The doughnut is a much more comprehensive, complex and accurate view of what would enable thriving people on a thriving planet than the singular measure of GDP. It brings to mind the old business adage, 'We value what we measure, and we measure what we value.' Until we start measuring all the categories that Raworth presents in the doughnut as a society, we are unlikely to really start valuing them, whether we are overshooting or in shortfall.

Let's look at how we could use the doughnut to help us create healthy limits as foundations for our own lives. If we add to the financial boundaries we've already considered following Charles Handy's lead, what other categories for our lives would enable us to thrive? Limits that, as we've established, far from restricting our possibilities, become healthy containers to enable us to flourish. Just as in Art 4, you created boundaries to enable the coherence you need for *doing* Enough in your life, now think about limits in relation to *having* Enough.

 PRACTICE 21: CREATE YOUR OWN 'ENOUGH DOUGHNUT'

1. Draw your own 'doughnut': two circles, one inside the other. In between the two circles is the doughnut itself – where what you have is Enough – the space where you personally thrive, living a creative, happy, successful life.

2. In the innermost circle, write down the things that are essential for you, in order for you to feel that you have enough to thrive.

   You could borrow from Raworth's categories and write down your personal minimum requirement for each that feels relevant to you. As a reminder, they are 'food, water, energy, networks, housing, gender equality, social equity, political voice, peace and justice, income and work, education and health'.

   It is more than likely that there are other things that are essential for you to thrive too. It may help to refer back to your values and purpose from Art 2. For me, including my values here felt essential, so I added them, with a sentence describing my minimum requirement for each one, in order to feel I have 'Enough'.

3. Beyond the outer rim of the doughnut, write down your own version of 'ecological ceiling'. This is where you set your intention about your own personal impact – your environmental footprint. How you choose to consume. This could be recycling, how you travel, what you choose to buy, what you choose to eat and charities you may support. This is the part of the doughnut where you can choose to set limits connected with your income as well as the impact that you have on the planet and her resources. This may already be really clear for you, or could be a new way of thinking. The invitation is for you to reflect on this for yourself and what it means for you.

It can be easy here to get distracted by judgement – by 'shoulds' or 'ought tos'. In an attempt to move away from this, when I did this part of the exercise, I set up three bits of paper on the floor called, 'head', 'heart' and 'gut'. I then went to each piece of paper and sensed into what I want my personal impact on the planet to be from a 'head' perspective, a 'heart' perspective and a 'gut' perspective. This led to powerfully different responses and helped me to connect to what I truly want for the world as well as what I want for me. It really did release me from any sense of being judged by myself or others – I invite you to do the same. After all, for us to feel the agency of our own limits, they have to feel true.

4. Now reflect on what life would be like for you living within the limits of the doughnut. A life of thriving within the enabling limits of Enough Growth.

Here visualization can help. Imagine a time when you are thriving. All is going well; you are living your values and your life has meaning. What is happening for you? What does it feel like to be here? Write down a description of what it is like. Again, this can be a wonderfully creative process, and can be informed by what you have learned about yourself in the other chapters. You are describing your life of 'Enough'. Inside my doughnut, I have sentences like, 'I belong here,' 'I am connected to others, living in community,' 'I have time to savour the world I live in,' 'I am working in flow,' 'I have time for all aspects of my life,' 'I am working with others to make a positive difference.'

5.   Now consider what it is that you could change in your life, connected to the resources that you already have, in order to get you to a place where you are meeting your fundamental needs without overshooting the healthy boundaries needed for your own sustainable life in a healthy planet?

This list can become the focus of your Enough Growth as you work towards living your life within your personal limits of Enough.

I'm not suggesting here that the task of re-balancing the massive imbalances in the global economy and the global environment is down to each of us personally. Without question, finding Enough Growth on a global scale so that humanity can live within the limits of the doughnut, where every person has enough and we don't exceed planetary boundaries, will require massive commitment and co-ordinated action from governments, corporations and industry. They (as we do) will need to adopt an Enough Mindset and take a view of the whole – perhaps even a shift in consciousness. Having said that, I believe that what each of us does in this space really does matter. How each of us chooses to live on the earth makes a difference, not just to the planet's survival but to the lives of others and our own lives. I believe that living a life of Enough Growth is as important for each of us and our well-being as it is for the planet. When we are filled with presence – conscious awareness of our agency and impact – we can choose to act in ways that really do make a difference and are profoundly fulfilling in their own right. That's certainly my experience anyway.

WHEN LESS IS MORE

One of the apparent paradoxes of the economics of the last 70 years, certainly in the Western economies of the global North, is that while the average individual wealth has continued to rise, people's happiness has not. Once described to me by environmentalist and author, Jonathon Porritt, as the 'crocodile graph', there are multiple examples from a range of countries that show the gap between rising wealth on the top line and the flatline of people's contentment on the bottom – making the graph look on the page like the wide-open mouth of a crocodile.

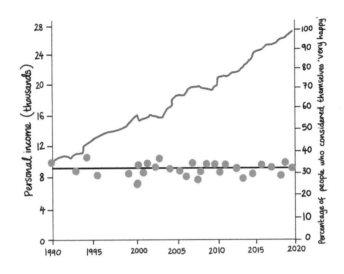

Many politicians, economists, psychologists and researchers have scratched their heads over this conundrum for years. I think it describes what we all know deep down: that once our basic needs are met, more wealth doesn't automatically make us happy. As Freud famously suggested, money doesn't make us happy because it doesn't fulfil an infantile wish in us. There is a whole happiness industry informed by years of research undertaken by hundreds of psychologists which can help us identify what *does* make us happy: intrinsic motivation, connection with others, vocation, purpose; attending to our body, mind and spirit. And what does this research tell us? Once we have enough wealth, more isn't the way to increase happiness.

More than that, even when we do have Enough wealth to meet our own needs, we can all be tipped off balance into Scarcity quickly by seeing that someone else has more than we do. This is brilliantly described by Kenneth Grahame in *The Wind in the Willows*.[16] One of the characters, 'the incorrigible

Mr Toad', is perfectly happy with his narrowboat until he sees a passing horse-drawn caravan and, having acquired one, he is happy enough with it until he sees a motor car – which he comically becomes obsessed with having. There is plenty of data confirming that the happiest nations are those with the smallest gap between the richest and poorest members of society. This is so entirely human and recognizable, and confirmed by what we know about our neurobiological make-up – we are hard-wired for fairness. As David Rock puts it in *Your Brain at Work*,[17] 'fairness is a primary need for the brain. A sense of fairness in and of itself can create a strong reward response, and a sense of unfairness can generate a threat response that lasts for days.' I am happy with my lot until I find out that you are getting more than me for the same effort. This is made worse by the fact that comparing ourselves with others is a particular challenge for our social media obsessed age, and as we know from statistics about mental health, rather than making us happier, it is actively harmful to many of us, as we'll explore in the next chapter.

What then, can this teach us in relation to Enough Growth? This simple fact: that comparison with others can push us off balance into a state of Scarcity, from which we may overcompensate and end up with more than we need – equally off balance in a state of Excess. One of the ways of re-balancing ourselves back to the state of Enough is by really appreciating and valuing what we have. When we focus on what we have and not on what we lack, we can cultivate gratitude, presence and intentionality. In her world-famous book, *Spark Joy*,[18] Marie Kondo sets out her principles of living a 'decluttered life'. Kondo suggests that we should only keep anything in our homes that is either useful or 'sparks joy'. I love Kondo's use of the word joy here. When she first rose to global fame, I suspect that this was what attracted so many people – Kondo isn't just offering us tidy homes; she is offering us joy in our lives. More than mere happiness, our lives can be surrounded by things that we love, appreciate and value. She describes it like this: 'When something sparks joy, you should feel a little thrill, as if the cells in your body are slowly rising.' This is wonderfully somatic and reminds us that joy isn't cerebral – we don't *think* joy, we *feel* it – and the source of that information resides in our whole bodies. Moreover, Kondo suggests that even when we are throwing away things that no longer have a use or give us joy, we do so with gratitude. She writes, 'By letting go of things that have been in your life with a feeling of gratitude, you foster appreciation for, and a desire to take better care of, the things in your life.' What becomes possible for us when we give ourselves this new space?

A friend of mine wrote to tell me about the impact of doing the Marie Kondo process on her house. She said:

> I got rid of between 20 and 40% of each category of my possessions. I don't miss anything, and I really wish I could have been more aware as I was accumulating stuff. I never think of myself as being materialistic but my cultural upbringing as a child of parents who lived through the war, and were therefore used to managing on very little, made it hard for me to let go of things in sufficient quantities. I had more than enough, and it had become overwhelming. Cutting back was liberating. Now I'm much more careful about what I acquire, which fits well with the sustainability agenda and treading more lightly on this earth.

The 'Sparks Joy' movement serves to remind us that having Enough is in part about what we value. And this doesn't have to be material things – it can be experiences too. If, like me, you have ever suffered from FOMO (the fear of missing out) then you might like to discover what the Australian poet Michael Leunig has called JOMO.[19] His poem sums it up perfectly:

> Oh the joy of missing out.
> When the world begins to shout
> And rush towards that shining thing;
> The latest bit of mental bling–
> Trying to have it, see it, do it,
> You simply know you won't go through it;
> The anxious clamouring and need
> This restless hungry thing to feed.
> Instead, you feel the loveliness;
> The pleasure of your emptiness.
> You spurn the treasure on the shelf
> In favour of your peaceful self;
> Without regret, without a doubt.
> Oh the joy of missing out.

When we are able to savour what we have, be it simply awareness of the present moment, a cup of tea, daffodils in spring, or something of particular beauty or functionality that you really value in your home, we enter into the state of Enough. Again, we return to the theme of being present – alert and aware to where we are and the choices available to us. Appreciating what we have in life, whether it is something within ourselves, our resource, our work, or a material object that we possess, opens our hearts to cultivating what matters. And in doing so we grow our capacity for Enough.

DREAMS OF TRANSFORMATION

With transformation comes wisdom – a knowledge drawn from within and gained from the depths of our experience. To transform, we need to drop into a state of openness and curiosity, so that we are able to widen our perspective – and include things that we have previously excluded. Perhaps things that we have overlooked or even thrown away – like imaginal cells, we may not have even known that they were there.

David Attenborough in his inspiring and heart-breaking film of 2020, *A Life on Our Planet*, offers his 'witness statement' to the world.[20] He is asked at the end what would make the biggest difference to the environmental crisis we face. His answer, 'less waste'. Attenborough is calling for an end to the 'take, make, use, lose' cycle and encouraging us, as we've explored in this chapter, to learn the value of living within the limits of the world's resources so that not only do we halt the climate catastrophe but reverse it. This will require a real shift in our individual and collective thinking – a transformation mindset if you will – a move from 'take, make' to re-use and regenerate. The final stage of the Enough Growth cycle invites us to tap into our potential for transforming how we live together on this planet.

To do this, we need to change how we view our raw materials. Instead of 'raw' materials that have never been used before – freshly mined, chopped down or drilled up – we start to use 'renewable' materials. Things that we have used and might previously have discarded, but now see as the basis for something new. We see them with 'new eyes' and get creative about how they can bring us value and utility. This goes way beyond the current practice of recycling packaging and 'waste products' and invites us to see everything that we throw away not as rubbish but as a resource. What might that look like in your life? What do you normally discount or discard that could actually be re-framed into a resource that could be used again or differently? Many of us will be used to re-using things – my house is full of empty jam jars ready for the next batch of chutney – and there is an entire design movement of people re-purposing furniture and upcycling.

This thinking is transforming the way that we can run the economy, manufacture our goods and harvest what we waste. In a wonderful synchronicity with our analogy of metamorphosis and transformation, this is a move from the linear, 'take, make, use, lose' economy, which looks like a caterpillar, to a 'circular economy', which has been modelled to look like a butterfly by the Ellen MacArthur Foundation.[21]

The circular economy is a major focus of research and innovation across the globe and is widely acknowledged as one of the ways in which the world can meet the emissions reductions commitments made by 195 countries worldwide in the UN's Paris Agreement signed in 2020. The reason I find this model so hopeful and exciting is because it's not just about doing less: it's about doing things differently. Kate Raworth calls it 'generous by design' – where we are not only trying to be carbon neutral, but actively doing things that give back to the planet, to others and by default to ourselves too.

In the face of huge systemic change, our challenge is to keep this feeling personal enough so we engage, rather than think of it as something that only others (governments, corporations, industry) can do. 'Generous by design' is a hook that works – it appeals to our higher selves – our values

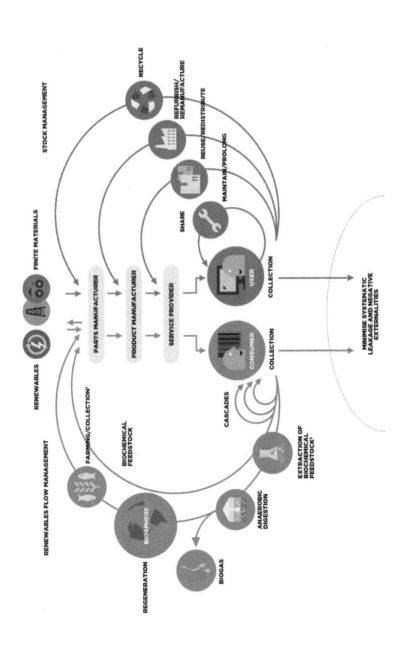

RENEWABLES FLOW MANAGEMENT

STOCK MANAGEMENT

FINITE MATERIALS

RENEWABLES

FARMING/COLLECTION¹

BIOCHEMICAL FEEDSTOCK

RECYCLE

REFURBISH/ REMANUFACTURE

REUSE/REDISTRIBUTE

MAINTAIN/PROLONG

SHARE

PARTS MANUFACTURER

PRODUCT MANUFACTURER

SERVICE PROVIDER

USER

CONSUMER

COLLECTION

COLLECTION

CASCADES

EXTRACTION OF BIOCHEMICAL FEEDSTOCK²

ANAEROBIC DIGESTION

BIOSPHERE

BIOGAS

REGENERATION

MINIMISE SYSTEMATIC LEAKAGE AND NEGATIVE EXTERNALITIES

and our creativity. It is also circular: generosity is reciprocal and therefore intrinsically satisfying. As nineteenth-century philosopher Jeremy Bentham put it:

> Create all the happiness you are able to create: remove all the misery you are able to remove. Every day will allow you to add something to the pleasure of others, or to diminish something of their pains. And for every grain of enjoyment you sow in the bosom of another, you shall find a harvest in your own bosom; while every sorrow which you pluck out from the thoughts and feelings of a fellow creature shall be replaced by a beautiful peace and joy in the sanctuary of your soul.[22]

Generosity is a close relation of gratitude and appreciation – the flow of giving and receiving. They feed off each other; both are sourced from a sense of abundance. When we are able to give something back to humanity or indeed the planet, we are practising a level of abundance that once again mirrors nature. This is why social justice and economic redistribution go hand in hand with environmental restoration. When we mimic the abundance and generosity of nature itself, not only do we make a positive difference, but we tap into something fundamental about ourselves. Writer Charles Eisenstein puts it like this:

> All beings yearn toward the exuberant expression of their life force. Birds sing much more than necessary; kittens play more than they have to; raspberries taste better than they need to. And you too, my friend, yearn to express your gifts in a beautiful way, more beautiful than necessary to secure a living.[23]

What would it be like to go beyond de-cluttering our own lives and to actively re-purpose what we are throwing away so that they can be useful to others? What would it give us to do more?

There are so many ways in which each of us can work on our own transformation and there are plenty of online resources and movements that offer us ideas about how to live generously for a thriving planet. There are increasing numbers of businesses too that set themselves up from the outset to be 'generous by design' – and more and more people are seeking them out – not just to buy their goods and services but to work with them. In her book *Powered by Purpose*,[24] Sarah Rozenthuler describes how six out of ten people in the millennial generation cite 'a sense of purpose' as key to them choosing what employer to work for. Purpose, as we know from Art 2, is found in part by connecting with your intrinsic motivation, and in part by connecting with others – making a contribution that is bigger than the individual benefits you may get from it. Increasingly, people are seeking ways to come together and not just work for a living, but work in order to give back, make a positive contribution to society.

The businesses that are modelling this vision of Enough Growth are thriving. From the clothing business Patagonia to the toilet paper company Who Gives a Crap, there are multiple examples of businesses that are shaping their offer, be it products or services, in the context of making a positive contribution by committing not just a slice of their profits, but activities that contribute to making things better, or by campaigning and using their platform to educate their consumers. This expands both our choices as consumers and our frame of what Enough Growth is. Not only can we choose to buy fewer products, but we now have a wide variety of choice about buying goods that make a positive contribution to the world we live in.

THE WISDOM OF ENOUGH GROWTH

Bringing the transformation stage of the Enough Growth cycle to life for you personally will almost certainly require you to look deep inside yourself, as well as reviewing the ways in which you live and work in the world we are currently the custodians of. Thinking about what it is that you habitually overlook or discard, which could instead be a resource for what you do next, may take time, and for me certainly, requires me to sit in the 'soup' of not knowing for a while. However, thinking about the resources that I have and how I can pass them on, or re-use them, gives me great pause for thought. How I pass on what I have learned along the way to others – 'sending the ladder back down'; how I use the resources I have generously; and how I turn my heartbreak to hope are all ways in which, for me, seeking Enough Growth has deep resonance. I believe that it is when we start to do this collectively that we may start to notice the transformation we long for. Personally, my 'Dream of Transformation' is when each of us can say, 'I am Enough,' 'I do Enough' and 'I have Enough,' so that we can, from a place of love, abundance and generosity, pour our collective energy into focusing on mutual flourishing, for ourselves, for each other and for the natural world.

SUMMARY OF *ENOUGH GROWTH*

- A new model for growth is needed so that we can find a sustainable way to flourish individually and collectively.
- Never-ending growth is a myth that doesn't make us happy.
- Within the healthy limits of Enough Growth we have freedom to focus on flourishing.
- Appreciating what we have brings joy.
- For us all to flourish, we need to think in terms of transformation – what is possible for us when we live within planetary means where everyone has what they need to thrive?
- Enough Growth draws on generosity and gratitude.
- Enough Growth harnesses our creativity and deepest sense of meaning so that we can transform to grow.

The transformative potential within Enough Growth is…

…accessing our wisdom

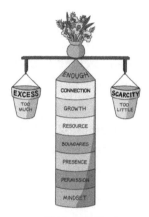

ART 7: ENOUGH CONNECTION

THE LOVE THAT GLUES ENOUGH TOGETHER

One touch of nature makes the whole world kin.

William Shakespeare[1]

In Art 7, we will explore the importance of relationship and connection, where we can find a healthy and sustainable balance in our world, together, drawing on the best of ourselves. As the world faces the challenge of our times – climate emergency and all the consequences of that – we consider how connecting in relationship with our deepest longing, each other and with nature is the key to us finding balance and agency to make the changes we need to.

We'll dive into:

- *the high cost of living in a culture of Scarcity;*
- *love – the power behind Enough Connection;*
- *'more in common': Enough Connection with each other;*
- *the future: safeguarding our descendants;*
- *nature: recovering our key relationship;*
- *connection as the foundation of having Enough.*

THE HIGH COST OF LIVING IN A CULTURE OF SCARCITY

When we look at the world around us, it is easy to see why so many of us get drawn into a state of Scarcity or Excess. Loneliness and isolation are on the rise in society, most intensely for younger and older generations. The way we have been required to live and work in the global pandemic has accelerated a move towards separation. Most of us live in cities, out of contact with the land, making it easy to forget how dependent we are on it for our survival. Little wonder that the climate catastrophe and ecological damage to much of the world's habitats are not the top priority for many. It all feels too remote and far away. The needs of the earth are disconnected from our lives just as we are disconnected from each other and even sometimes from ourselves. Let's explore the cost of living in this culture of Scarcity before we look at how we can re-balance and find Enough Connection.

For most of us in the third decade of the twenty-first century, our primary means of connecting is digital. This is not a bad thing in and of itself – far from it! Digital platforms and social media have been a blessing in the time of Covid-19 – they have kept us connected in a way that would have been impossible even 20 years earlier. But there is a cost to us connecting in this way. It is very easy to forget how to be Enough when we lack human, in-person connection. We can easily get tipped into comparing ourselves with others, or just forgetting the human need for relationship at work when our days are filled with back-to-back online meetings.

While social media can be a wonderful way of people finding connection and networks, it can also be a cruel place, full of comparison, judgement and even, in some cases, anonymized hate. This is so psychologically unsafe for us, it is no wonder we are triggered into a state of Scarcity. The only logical response is to protect ourselves by only sharing with others edited highlights of our lives. When this happens, it's the opposite of connection. We can't risk being our authentic selves, so we offer an idealized version – all jazz hands and smiles – where we have to be 'amazing', 'incredible', 'best ever', 'awesome!' In presenting only this side of ourselves to the world, we risk becoming disconnected from our inner voice, our inner guidance and our inner lives. It can feel to some that who we *really* is and what we *really* feel is too shameful or unshareable for the outside world, unless it serves a story about recovery when we can triumphantly declare ourselves to be cured. This has a high cost for us because it can tip us into shame. Brene Brown, who researches and writes extensively about shame and vulnerability says, 'shame is the fear of disconnection – it's the fear that something we've done or failed to do, an ideal that we've not lived up to, or a goal that we've not accomplished, makes us unworthy of connection. *I'm not worthy or good enough for love, belonging or connection.*[2] This is a painful lived experience for many – connection and belonging that feel so conditional and driven by fear that they can't be trusted. It's a lonely place to be.

There is a cost of disconnection in our workplaces too. During the global pandemic, as the world transferred to online platforms to connect and do business, we lost human connection. Meetings lost the social interaction at the start. No one bumped into anyone in the office corridors anymore. No more small talk and gossip in those 'water-cooler moments'. Instead, people logged on, cracked through the agenda and logged off again, often with barely a moment to breathe before the next online meeting. It took a while to realize that in losing the relational side of human interaction, we were foregoing fundamental human needs. Without connecting with one another, there was no pause in the often relentlessness of each day. No time to exhale together in a moment of shared reflection over a cup of tea. It is in these moments that we connect, not just to our shared work, but our shared experience of working together.

Let me give you an example of this. About five months into the pandemic, I was asked to run a session with an executive team who had been operating in crisis mode for months. Everyone was exhausted and working incredibly hard. I asked the team how often they had managed to check in on each other since the crisis began. Despite the fact that they were meeting three times a week, their response was, 'we haven't'. So we spent the first half of the team day together simply inviting each person to talk about how they were. People shared fears, vulnerabilities, concerns and achievements with each other. They talked openly about their personal feelings, their families and how they found working in this way. As the morning went on, it was clear just how much everyone needed to talk about these things, and how much they had missed being able to connect with each other – to be seen and heard at a human level. The impact was palpable, and it was a powerful realization for all of us. Connection is not just a nice thing to have: it's essential for well-being. It takes time, and it's time well spent – however much is on the agenda. Members of that team told me several weeks after the session how much it had made a difference not only to how they felt, but to how they worked together. They found ways to collaborate again – and group planning became easier – underpinned by a revived collective sense of belonging to each other in a team.

Now, let's turn to look at the cost of disconnection with the land and the cycles of nature. We've all heard stories of urban children the world over, often living in areas of deprivation, who have no clue that milk comes from cows, eggs from chickens or even chips from potatoes. While we can shake our heads at the disconnection that this symbolizes, how many of us are really aware of the extent to which rainforests in South America (sometimes called the lungs of the earth) are being felled to plant soya to feed chicken and cattle to supply wealthier countries with meat in the quantities and at the price they've come to expect it? As more and more of the world migrates to live in cities (in 2020, 74.9% of Europeans and 83.6% of North Americans were urban dwellers and the percentage of urban dwellers is increasing the world over),[3] we risk becoming increasingly disconnected from the land that we come from – the natural world that is our shared home. This is so much more than a question of knowledge about how our food is created. It's a fundamental risk of losing our connection with nature.

E.M. Forster wrote in his novel, *Howards End*, 'Only connect... live in fragments no longer.'[4] There is a very real need for each of us, in our own lives and collectively, to find connection on many levels, so that we can shift the balance away from Scarcity and Excess and back to Enough. None of us can solve the world's challenges alone, but when we connect with our heart's desires, with each other, and with the natural world, we can give it our best shot.

LOVE: THE POWER BEHIND ENOUGH CONNECTION

Having explored the high cost of disconnection, let's look at what's to be gained by learning the art of Enough Connection. Connection, as we have seen, is relational and essential for our survival – and our most important relationships have their foundation in love. I find Brene Brown's definition of connection really resonates. She describes it as: 'the energy that exists between people when they feel seen, heard, and valued; when they can give and receive without judgment; and when they derive sustenance and strength from the relationship.'[5] That sounds a lot like love to me. In *Power and Love: A Theory and Practice of Social Change*, Adam Kahane cites a definition of love as: 'the drive towards the unity of the separated'. Kahane goes on to say, 'love in this sense is the drive to reconnect and make whole that which has become or appears fragmented.'[6]

In order to move from the culture of Scarcity and Excess we currently inhabit, to one powered by Enough, we need not just to connect but to re-connect. We are in part remembering what we need to be fully human and how much difference it makes to us being able to live fruitfully. Re-connecting to what matters – in ourselves, with others and of course with how we live on this beautiful planet – means that we will have to come together again. This reminds me of the beautiful Japanese art of Kintsugi, where broken crockery is glued together using gold. There is no attempt to cover up the breakage; the reverse is true: the gold holding the broken fragments together is what makes the object beautiful in a new way. This lovingly crafted re-connected pottery is a great image for Enough Connection where the connection has become an integral part of the art. When we re-connect to parts of our lives that have become fragmented, we are honouring a deep human need: to be whole, held in relationship with others, glued together by love.

If we accept that at the core of Enough Connection is love, then in order to live authentic, full lives in a state of Enough, we need self-love. The writer bell hooks, in *All about Love*, explains why this is so important.[7]

> Self-love is the foundation of our loving practice. Without it our other efforts to love fail. Giving ourselves love we provide our inner being with the opportunity to have the unconditional love we may have always longed to receive from someone else... When we give this precious gift to ourselves, we are able to reach out to others from a place of fulfilment and not from a place of lack.

To use our framework, when we connect to ourselves with self-love, we return to a state of *being* Enough, as opposed to coming from a place of Scarcity, as we explored in the first part of this book. Connecting to a deep inner sense that we are loved, loveable and Enough means that we can reach out to connect with others, rather than constantly trying to compensate for something that we don't have. I'm wary of making conditional statements about the need for inner coherence being a prerequisite for outer coherence. It's not always sequential and there isn't always a conditional clause. But it is certainly true that we need to attend to both. In my experience, if I am feeling a lack of self-worth – not Enough, or somehow inadequate – it is harder for me to really connect to someone else. Which is why believing that we *are* Enough is so important: when we know we are Enough – *that we are worthy of belonging and of love* – we are able to forge new belongings in different places. Enough Connection gives us the gift of fullness, from which we are able to extend outwards. When we love ourselves, we are able to love others and vice versa.

'MORE IN COMMON': ENOUGH CONNECTION WITH EACH OTHER

Finding Enough Connection can require a shift in perspective – a more expansive concept of who we can connect with. One that adopts a sense of shared responsibility for the challenges we face in the twenty-first century; one that focuses on what connects us, rather than what separates us. As the late UK MP Jo Cox famously said, 'We are far more united and have far more in common with each other than things that divide us.'[8] When we are able to see and connect to each other's shared humanity, we can move beyond the things that keep us separate. In the 1990s in Northern Ireland, during the Truth and Reconciliation process, there was a rule that during the breaks people could only speak to each other about their families. This was a deliberate attempt to encourage people to focus on what they had in common, and it reportedly had a profound effect.

In the face of the huge imbalances that we face in our world in the first quarter of the twenty-first century, the populations of many countries across the world are frequently characterized as divided between two oppositional (and to some extent timeless) world views. One is the need to look out for ourselves to survive and protect ourselves from others; the second is the need for us to look out for each other and work together. Increasingly these two views are claimed by political positions – the right and left – and the entrenched division and polarization that we see in our societies is often drawn along these lines.

The dream of Enough Connection is that we can move beyond seeing these two world views in binary opposition, and to try instead to understand where each is coming from, because we need to include both. I find it useful to think of these two world views in relation to two essential parts of each of us. Robert Dilts (founder of NLP) describes people as having 'two complementary aspects: the ego and the soul. The ego is oriented toward survival, recognition and ambition,' which chimes with the isolationist world view, and 'The soul is oriented toward purpose, contribution and mission,' which chimes with a more global world view. He goes onto suggest that for individuals, 'Charisma, passion and presence emerge naturally when these two forces are aligned.'[9] In the same way that Dilts is suggesting, we need to find internal integration: how would it be if we could acknowledge the benefit and human need of both these world views, and harness them together in service of finding a solution to the global imbalances and climate catastrophe we face? In our search to *have* Enough in the world for its (and our) long-term survival, the more we can seek integration, connection and alignment the better.

In today's discourse, there is a strong risk of finding ourselves in echo chambers (especially online), where we only connect with people who are 'like us' – which leads to much of the division and factionalism that we see in the world today. For us to find Enough Connection, we need to look outwards and connect with others that we may not know or even agree with. The challenge of *having* Enough in the world, where we are sharing the resources of the planet within those all-important planetary limits that we explored in the last chapter, requires us to connect in the service of something bigger than all of us. And to do that, we need to start connecting more widely and having conversations that matter, not just with people who already share our view – but with those who don't.

 PRACTICE 22: SEEK DIFFERENCE

This practice sounds simple but can require a great deal of courage.

- Try seeking out someone who is outside of your normal circle of people that has different views or life experiences from you.

- Have a conversation with them about something that matters to them – perhaps in relation to the Art of Enough. The challenge is to have a good conversation without getting drawn into binary positions, in which you both end up re-stating your already strongly held positions.
- Seek to really listen to their view – so that you understand where they are coming from even if you don't agree with it.
- Reflect on how it felt to connect in this way. What was the cost, and what was the gain for you, and for them?

We need to re-find the ability to have conversations and debates with people who have different views, because until then, we will not be able to harness the best of ourselves in service of the challenges we all face. Years of supporting people in organizations to have conversations that matter when the stakes are high and they disagree has taught me that good conversations happen when:

- each person feels *psychologically safe* – this is what can be achieved by connecting with each other on a human level;
- establishing a level of *courtesy and respect* for the conversation – this is often non-verbal, and relates to tone of voice, body language and even the environment;
- each person feels *seen and heard* – both parties listen well and ask open questions;
- both parties agree a *shared purpose* for the conversation which keeps it anchored in shared interest;

- both parties *avoid point scoring* and resist the temptation to get drawn into winning the argument.

The most successful organizational leaders that I've worked with are those that focus on creating a shared purpose – a vision that people can get behind, despite their differences. And it feels good individually too, being part of something greater than us. When I move my thinking from a focus on 'me' to a focus on 'we', I immediately find myself moving into a different energy – one of service and connection (from ego to soul). This outward motion connects me to my purpose and my values and increases my sense of agency and ability to get things done. And as it turns out, it's not that hard. In fact, it's a fundamental part of our make-up. The fallacy that we are instinctively selfish and individualistic as a species has been well and truly de-bunked. Kate Raworth puts it like this: 'Homo sapiens, it turns out, is the most co-operative species on the planet, out-performing ants, hyenas and even the naked mole-rat when it comes to living alongside those who are beyond our next of kin.'[10] When we focus our energy and attention on connecting with each other and working together, we are also connecting to a deep-seated part of who we are by nature.

When we see we are part of the whole, not only individuals within it, we make different decisions. We connect ourselves not only to each other but to being part of the solution. As anthropologist Margaret Mead famously said, 'Never doubt that a small group of thoughtful, committed citizens can change the world; indeed it is the only thing that ever has.' I find this such an encouraging thought because it reminds us that even though the scale and size of the challenges we face can feel enormous, actually the small things we do in community with others really can have an impact. The small-scale, grass-roots, collaborative community acts that people across the globe are engaged in really do make a difference. In *Local is Our Future: Steps to an Economics of Happiness*,[11] author and film-maker Helena Norberg-Hodge suggests small local initiatives are exactly where we should be looking to make a difference to the big systemic challenges. It's not only more sustainable – it is beneficial for our well-being too. She says: 'People are coming to recognize that connection, both to others and to Nature herself, is the wellspring of human happiness. And every day new, inspiring initiatives are springing up that offer the potential for genuine prosperity.'

THE FUTURE: SAFEGUARDING OUR DESCENDANTS

For us to find Enough Connection so that we can live together on the planet in a sustainable way, and all thrive long term, it can also help us to re-evaluate our relationship with the future. In *The Good Ancestor: How to Think Long Term in a Short-Term World*,[12] Roman Krznaric argues that we need to start to connect more with the future and specifically our (collective) descendants. Helpfully, he offers 'six ways to think long':

- Deep-time humility: grasp we are an eyeblink in cosmic time.
- Legacy mindset: be remembered well by posterity.
- Intergenerational justice: consider the seventh generation ahead.
- Cathedral thinking: plan projects beyond a human lifetime.

- Holistic forecasting: envision multiple pathways for civilization.
- Transcendent goal: strive for one-planet thinking.

The really striking thing about this way of framing the changes we need to make to how we live is that in order to ensure that our children and children's children don't live with too little, we need to stop having too much now. Finding the Art of Enough now will mean that future generations will be able to have Enough as well. It's as if we spin the scales in a new direction to accommodate a new time dimension. When we start to think like 'good ancestors', we immediately have to think beyond the span of our own lifetimes – the ultimate exercise in moving beyond our own egos. Once again, we are invited to see beyond ourselves and our own needs, and move into a generous, service mentality – where we live our lives driven by what we can contribute to the greater whole, rather than simply what we need for ourselves. In this way, finding Enough Connection with our descendants can inspire us to find Enough in our own lives.

I am particularly struck when taking the time perspective by how much we have disconnected from the sense of stewardship for our own people and indeed our environment. We have lost what so many of our ancestors had – the sense of creating something for posterity. Since World War Two, our focus has become increasingly more immediate and less concerned about creating a lasting legacy for those who come after. Long-term thinking is a strong philosophy held by indigenous tribes the world over. The Iroquois of North America founded their Confederacy in the twelfth century on the principle of leading with seven generations in mind. Just as they honour and pay homage to seven generations of ancestors, all decisions they make have to consider the impact on their people and the land for seven generations into the future – about 140 years. This Apache saying puts it beautifully: 'We do not inherit the land from our ancestors; we borrow it from our children.'[13]

It requires a really good imagination to think in this way, and it can be a powerful exercise. When I look back at the family tree my uncle has lovingly taken years to collate, I can imagine the lives of my forebears. I can, with some historical context and surviving evidence (old photos, diaries, letters), build a picture of the lives that came before me. I can connect and honour them by imagining some of their joys, hardships and life experience. It's a bit more of a leap to cast my mind into the future – there are so many variables, and for me at least, it can feel like a bit of a sci-fi activity. Nonetheless, I can usually get to three generations – imagining what it might be like for my daughters, nieces and nephews and any children they might have. It gives me pause, and really activates my sense of responsibility about the decisions, big and small, that I make in my life. I have the sense of passing the baton on. Receiving what I've been given from the generations before and making my contribution to those that come after. I like this sense of symmetry: it gives me a deep sense of ease and meaning.

 PRACTICE 23: LETTER TO YOUR DESCENDANTS

- Write a letter to one of your descendants to read in fifty or even a hundred years' time, explaining what you did in order to have Enough in the early twenty-first century.

- Reflecting on your letter, what impact does this have on how you are living now and the daily decisions you are making?
- What could you change about how you are living that would ensure that your descendants have Enough?

Many environmentalists have been advocating for years that we need to revive the notion of stewardship to inform our decision making and protect the legacy of future generations. As Krznaric reminds us, we have not always been so pre-occupied with the short term. There have been many times in history when people have engaged in what he calls 'cathedral thinking', where they start a project that will never be complete in their lifetimes. What would that be for you? For us? Looking forward to our descendants in this way reminds us once again that love is at the root of Enough Connection. When we imagine the people (our collective grand-children and great grand-children) who will be living with the consequences of our decisions today, it may be easier for us connect to them and their lives with a sense of love – wanting them to be well and happy. And this gives our decision making a different focus.

Holocaust survivor and psychologist Victor Frankl, in *Man's Search for Meaning*,[14] offers an insight that for me speaks profoundly to this need for long-term thinking and Enough Connection. He suggests that we cannot be free unless we are also responsible – the two are intrinsically connected. He says:

Freedom is only part of the story and half of the truth... In fact, freedom is in danger of degenerating into mere arbitrariness unless it is lived in terms of responsibility. That is why I recommend that the Statue of Liberty on the East Coast (of USA) be supplemented by a Statue of Responsibility on the West Coast.

What a symbol that would be! A Statue of Responsibility in the 'Land of the Free' to remind us that we are connected to one another, to the land, to our ancestors and descendants and that we are collectively responsible not only to each other but for looking after the planet while we are here.

Any historian will tell you that the benefit of looking back is to learn the lessons in the present that will help us build a better future. It feels as if we are at a seminal time in the early twenty-first century, where the hard-won lessons of countless generations of people the world over are at risk of being forgotten, in favour of the immediate short-term gain that we focus on. The invitation for each of us is to re-connect with our collective sense of responsibility, stewardship and legacy, in order to find Enough not only in our lives but those of the generations to come. What difference would this perspective make to the way we live, work, lead others and lead our lives?

NATURE: RECOVERING OUR KEY RELATIONSHIP

At the commencement address at Berkeley College of Natural Resources in 2005, Chief Oren Lyons of Iroquois Onondaga Nation said this: 'What you call resources, we call our relatives. If you can think in terms of relationships, you are going to treat them better aren't you? Get back to the relationship because that is your foundation for survival.'[15] This thinking, that centuries ago people across the world shared, now requires a paradigm shift for us in the West. From the planet comprising inanimate natural resources for us to 'use', 'own' or 'exploit', to something that we have a deeply felt connection with. Again, with this approach we bring ourselves back to 'we' not 'I'. We move beyond a transactional understanding of the world, which is fundamentally fragmented – to a relational one, in which we are all connected.

It's so deeply ironic that pretty much all of us (and I include myself in this) will marvel at the beauty of a sunset over the sea or sunlight streaming through a dappled forest, or stand in awe at the sight of a murmuration of starlings, at the same time as inadvertently doing or eating or using something every single day of our lives that is harmful to the planet. Our way of living is so deeply disconnected from planetary well-being that it can sometimes be hard to fathom how to re-connect with the natural world and live in partnership with it. It certainly requires collective purpose and action. And once again, it requires love. Charles Eisenstein puts it like this:

> Earth is alive. What is alive, we can love. What we love, we wish to serve. When what we love is sick, we want to ease its suffering and serve its healing. The more deeply we know it, the better we can join its healing.[16]

We need to fall back in love with nature. Really connect, so that we understand ourselves as being in relationship with it, prioritising its on-going flourishing. Just as self-love can be the key to unlocking a sense of Enough Connection with ourselves, so love for nature is the key for Enough Connection with the planet. The wholeness and healing that so many of us crave in our lives is mirrored in the wholeness and healing that our planet so badly needs right now.

This may sound fanciful and unscientific. It is certainly a move away from the mechanistic science that powered the Western agricultural and industrial revolutions. In fact though, it is in tune with the newer scientific understanding of the world, informed by the discoveries of quantum physics, that tell us that the world is made up of living atoms. It invokes the concept of Gaia described in the Introduction, where we understand that the world is deeply interconnected: that what happens in one part of the world has an impact on the other side of the globe.

Taking a meta view, for the last four hundred years, the Western world has been dominated by a mindset that is rational, scientific and material. This has led, of course, to great developments and a wonderful enriching of human life in many ways. But it has been at the cost of excluding the natural world and our relationship with it. It has driven the separation of people from nature, and the sense that the planet is ours to own and use. It has led to a separation of head (our rationality), heart (our relationships) and gut (our instinct). The rational has dominated all: emotions and relationships have been less valued and less important than ideas and intellect, and instinct has been all but ignored as an irrelevant human quality. As we have explored, this has been damaging both to the world and to us, and the movement that is now required is one of re-integration – with ourselves and with nature. To quote Eisenstein again, 'it is time to recognise ourselves as the connected living self in co-creative partnership with the earth.' As we re-balance ourselves – find the Art of Enough – we can re-balance our relationship with our shared home. We can re-integrate the natural world as an active part of our lives.

How can we do this? In order to really engage and connect with these big questions, we need to tether ourselves to something that is real and tangible for us. We need to be grounded – connected with Mother Earth. Otherwise, we risk getting lost in abstractions, or in telling others what to do. We risk tipping into overwhelm and a state of Excess and losing connection with the humanity at the heart of what's required of us. Finding our own felt relationship with nature is really important and, of course, highly personal. Once again, what starts as an individual connection ripples out in how we live and work with our families, organizations and communities. Below are some simple activities that can re-kindle our Enough Connection with nature. Simple by design, they are rooted in the concept of appreciation for the present moment.

 PRACTICE 24: CONNECTING WITH NATURE

- Plant a seed and nurture it to life. I always find it astonishing how much this kindles feelings of care, compassion and pride.
- Lie on the earth on a sunny day.
- Simply stand barefoot outside, feeling the earth beneath your feet and the sky above you.
- Sit by, or swim in, some water – a river, pool, the sea.
- Seek out a place where your relationship with nature comes alive and give yourself regular time to visit it.

Personally, I find it a deeply resourcing, soulful practice to have time in nature every day. I'm lucky to live by the River Thames in Oxford, which I run along each morning. Sometimes in winter I'm running under the stars with the trees silhouetted against the night sky. In spring, it is lighter and each year I experience again the thrill of new buds, catkins and bulbs. In the summer, by the time I run, the dawn is long gone and I'm catching the coolness of a hot day. In the autumn, my favourite horse chestnut tree offers up its beautiful conkers – I still have the childlike excitement of picking up a conker or two and putting it in my pocket, marvelling at the intricacy and polish of the markings. If I am lucky, I see the flash of a kingfisher and it literally takes my breath away; I see it as a blessing – nature reminding me in an iridescent burst of blue of her abundance. My lived experience is that in having this daily, half-hour connection with nature, I am more able to connect with myself, with others and with making a positive contribution in the world. It is simultaneously grounding and inspiring. I believe that however we are able to find time to connect to nature, it is something that enriches us in the moment and resources us longer term.

Fundamentally, to find the Art of Enough collectively, we need to value our Connection with nature. It is a relationship, and like any relationship or connection, it thrives when it is in balance – when we give as much as we receive. Luckily, we are not starting from scratch – far from it. There are long-standing and growing movements of people the world over who live and work in Connection with the earth and are already paving the way for us to create long-term, sustainable change. I'll mention just two as they give us such hope.

- The Great Green Wall in the Sahara Desert is a project run by the African Union, which plans to plant trees over 8,000 km – the width of Africa – by 2030. Once it's finished it will be the largest living structure on the planet. 'The Wall promises to be a compelling solution to the many urgent threats not only facing the African Continent, but the global community as a whole – notably climate change, drought, famine, conflict and migration.'[17]
- Tree Sisters is an organization that supports women in communities living with the impact of deforestation to plant trees.[18] They fund education, training and trees for women to re-forest their local environments – specifically in areas that need tropical reforestation. Their vision is for 'a world in which it is normal for everyone to protect and restore themselves and their world.'

Rather wonderfully, we can take our cues from nature herself for how to step back from the brink of environmental collapse and regenerate the eco-systems that have been destroyed. Janine Benyus is a biomimicry designer. Biomimicry is a new discipline within science and design that sources inspiration from the eco-systems and patterns in nature. Benyus says this:

In the natural world the definition of success is the continuity of life… life has learned to create conditions conducive to life. That's really the magic heart of it. And that's also the design brief for us right now. We have to learn how to do that.[19]

Taking this concept as an inspiration, what would it mean in our individual and collective lives if our aim of living and working well together was to 'create conditions conducive to life'? What a powerful way to anchor our shared endeavours. Helena Norberg-Hodge describes how this is already happening:

> Around the world we are witnessing a truly positive cultural evolution. We are re-learning what ancient indigenous cultures knew: that the 'inner' and the 'outer', and the human and the non-human, are inextricably intertwined. We are beginning to see the world within us – to experience more consciously the great interdependent web of life, of which we ourselves are part.[20]

For me, this is the definition of Enough Connection.

CONNECTION AS THE FOUNDATION TO HAVING ENOUGH

Enough Connection provides a solution-focused orientation, where from a place of being Enough, with others, in service of our descendants, all can thrive. Over the next few decades, humankind is going to have to change – to avoid catastrophic climate events and ecocide. If we can do this from a place of Enough Connection – in relationship with our own deepest longing, in relationship with each other and in relationship with nature herself, it will be such a rewarding journey. We will be able to move away from focusing on *having* Enough in relation to cost and what we have to stop, and turn instead towards focusing on what Enough gives us. Love is the glue that connects us, so that from a place of being, doing and having Enough we can live abundant lives together – sowing the seeds of Enough for generations to come.

SUMMARY OF *ENOUGH CONNECTION*

- Our culture of Scarcity leads to disconnection and loneliness.
- Connection is the life blood that runs through all human relationships.
- Connecting with ourselves is an act of self-love – and it enables us to connect with others.
- We need to connect with other people around our shared purpose, extending beyond our echo chambers.
- When we remember that we have more in common than what divides us, we are more able to find Connection.
- Connecting with our ancestors and descendants reminds us that we are stewards of the earth and her resources, and that we want to be able to pass on the abundance we have experienced.
- Connecting with nature is a resource for us individually and a necessity for us collectively, so that we can co-create a sustainable future for us all.

The transformative potential within Enough Connection is...

...love, for yourself, for others, for our world

EPILOGUE

ENOUGH TRANSFORMATION

Come to the edge he said. They said, 'we are afraid'.
Come to the edge he said. They came. He pushed
them, and they flew.

Guillaume Apollinaire

Journeying through the seven Arts has led us to explore how
we can live with the Art of Enough from the inside out. We
have looked at how we can balance our inner state, our outer
lives and the wider world that we share. My hope is that you
will have found the part of the book that helps you to find
Enough where you most need it so that you can thrive and
shine in your world.

Each one of us will be drawn to different Arts – and
sometimes, we re-visit them at different points in our lives.
They are not sequential – more like a staircase that we go up
and down several times, stopping at different points along
the way. None of the work of finding the Art of Enough is
static. It requires constant effort and attention, and we'll

need to focus on different Arts at different times. For me, it's often several times a day. Whichever Art resonates for you, my vision is that the Art of Enough can be a launch pad for us to flourish in ways that we so desperately need in the early twenty-first century.

Sometimes we know where we are headed, and other times we have to let it emerge. Returning to the image of the caterpillar and butterfly that has run through this book, I wonder if each of us, in learning to be, do and have Enough, can also find our own personal transformation, which, when we are connected, will lead to the transformation of our world.

Let's remind ourselves of the imaginal cells that lie at the heart of each of the Arts:

Within Enough Mindset lies *abundance*.
Within Enough Permission we find *freedom*.
Within Enough Presence there lies *flow*.
Within Enough Boundaries we find *clarity*.
Within Enough Resource lives *power*.
Within Enough Growth we find *wisdom*.
Within Enough Connection we find *love*.

Throughout this book, we've used the Art of Enough model – a set of scales where Enough is balanced between Scarcity and Excess. I have an image, as we reach the end of this book, of the model itself transforming into the butterfly. The spine of the model turns, like a caterpillar, into a chrysalis, drawing on the imaginal cells within each Art – before becoming a butterfly. As the butterfly wings slowly unfurl, we see that Excess has been replaced by Love and Scarcity by Abundance.

Between the two wings is the body of Enough, where we are free, in flow, with clarity, power and wisdom.

My dream is that in finding our Art of Enough from the inside out, we are able to transform our lives, our work and our world into the beautiful and sustainable world we all know is possible. When we learn to believe that we are Enough, we do Enough, we have Enough, we can flourish, fulfil our potential and live as stewards of the planet we share – thriving together.

AN *ENOUGH* VISUALIZATION

I offer you this final visualization as a way of imagining your own transformation sourced by the Art of Enough.

Imagine yourself, in a state of Enough, walking towards the edge of a cliff. In front of you, beyond the big drop, is the most expansive landscape – a scene that is teeming with life and beauty. It is inviting you to be part of it, to offer yourself so that you too can contribute to this generative, sustainable world. As you stand there you breathe deeply. With each breath you feel into the abundance of your life; you breathe in your freedom; you feel centred, balanced, in flow; you draw on the clarity of purpose and the power of your resource; you tap into your wisdom and feel the love of your connection. Then you take a deep breath, close your eyes and trusting you will find the place where all can flourish together, you step forward and let your wings carry you on the wind.

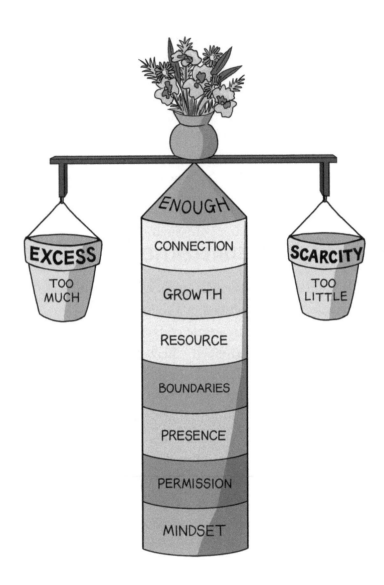

GLOSSARY OF PRACTICES

Bringing together each leaf and flower you have collected from the practices throughout the book.

ART 1

Practice 1: Appreciation
Practice 2: Asking incisive questions
Practice 3: Patterns of self-talk
Practice 4: Observing emotions

ART 2

Practice 5: Rules of belonging
Practice 6: Hidden loyalties
Practice 7: Permission slips
Practice 8: Core purpose
Practice 9: Values

ART 3

Practice 10: Coherent breathing
Practice 11: Positivity portfolio

ART 4

Practice 12: Enough Boundary #1: What matters most
Practice 13: Map your energy
Practice 14: Enough Boundary #2: Energy patterns
Practice 15: 'Stop doing' list
Practice 16: Keep a 'no' journal
Practice 17: Enough Boundary #3: Protect your time and focus

ART 5

Practice 18: The Wheel of Enough
Practice 19: Integrating your shadow
Practice 20: Working pattern review

ART 6

Practice 21: Create your own 'Enough Doughnut'

ART 7

Practice 22: Seek difference
Practice 23: Letter to your descendants
Practice 24: Connecting with nature

All these practices and more are available for download on the Art of Enough website:
www.theartofenough.co.uk

ACKNOWLEDGEMENTS

This book has been a long time coming. I first had the idea in 2013 and since then have been researching it and collecting stories, case studies and examples. Much of the source material for this book has been the inspirational, dedicated and wonderful clients that I have had the privilege to work with over 20 years. I am grateful to all of them for inviting me into their worlds and sharing their experiences with me. In addition, I would like to thank the many people who responded to online surveys and conversations, and those who offered me their personal experience and examples of Enough, especially: Sarah Thomson, Bernadette Cagnoni, Liz Curran, Pari Namaze, Neil Gore, Hugh Digby-Baker, Alli Spargo, Ria Knowles, Louise Parsons, Christopher Hall, Sarah Vokes-Tilley, Kit Mills, Lorna Durrant, Sally Northeast, Liz Goold, Kate Gittins, Erika Poole, Katherine Taylor-Birnie, Aurelian Koch, Maggie Saunders, John Watters, Chris Hall, Janice Keyes, Emma Webb, Roz Stevens, Suzanne Maxted, Michele Enright, Abi Harris, Pete Bone, Jayne Harrison and Megan Pengelly.

I have been blessed by people who have been prepared to talk through ideas, read drafts, and give me invaluable feedback as the book has been born. My huge thanks to Suzanne Raitt, Vee Pollock, Alison Vickers, Claire White, Ruth Overton, Laura Beckingham, Sarah Compton, Mary

McCammon and Sarah Wilkinson for being early readers of the book and helping it take shape. My parents, John and Tricia Hall-Matthews, also read early drafts; it was Mum who first told me about imaginal cells and instilled in me her love of nature (though sadly I don't share her encyclopaedic knowledge of it!). Gus Stewart and John Fielding introduced me to the world of psychotherapy, particularly the work of Donald Winnicott, Marion Milner and Carl Jung and set me on the journey of believing I could be 'good enough' 30 years ago. Thank you.

I owe an enormous debt of gratitude to the wise and soulful Michael Cahill, who read every single draft of this book as it emerged, and whose influence is on every page. Thank you, Michael, for the depth and generosity you showed me, and for the wide-ranging generative conversations we shared as this book took form – they were as enjoyable as the writing itself!

So many people supported me to keep writing by their on-going interest, encouragement, prompts, friendship and sometimes the no-nonsense 'just get on with it' advice that was needed. Charles Handy and his late wife, Liz Handy, offered great advice and encouragement about writing, as did Simon Mayo, Martin Wroe and Sarah Rozenthuler. Special thanks also to Rebecca Phillips, Iona Kenrick, Mathew Gibson, Euton Daley, Omar Wilkinson, Malou Ericsson, Saranne Postans, Jo Colville, Cynthia Hamilton, Alice Sheldon, Catherine Weetman, Ken Dickson, Louise Wiles, Andy Brookes, Oana Tanase, Chris Burton, Ceri Evans, Jeff Humm, Rhian Roberts, Susie and Crispin Holland, Clare Hall-Matthews, David Hall-Matthews, Liz Davidson, Jo De Waal, Bec Hill and Ian Denley. I am so grateful for my band:

Sarah Spackman, Clare White, Emma Stokes, Vanessa Eade, Caroline Krantz, Julian Followell and Hugo Shelton, for friendship, laughter and, of course, music.

I am lucky to have had many incredible teachers. I would like to thank John Whittington, Lynn Stoney and Dan Booth Cohen for what they have taught me about systemic consciousness and enabling the flow of life and love. My coach supervisor Katherine Long provides on-going wisdom and insight, Gavin Andrews trained me in HeartMath, and my yoga teachers Katie Phelps, Susanne Kaesbauer and Laurene Vetterli continue to teach me so much about the embodied practices of Enough. Deep thanks to all of you.

Alison Jones was the person who enabled this book to turn from 'the book I'm going to write one day' into the book that I have written. I feel so lucky to have had her guidance and support. Alison believed in *The Art of Enough* from the early stages and I'm thrilled to be publishing it with the fantastic Practical Inspiration Publishing. A massive thanks is also due to Daisy Mojave Holland for her fabulous illustrations and her patience with every iteration of them!

Finally, heartfelt thanks to Keeley Addison for daily chats, love, encouragement and just being there; Judy Parke for lifelong friendship, wit and wisdom; and my family who put up with me when I am in Excess and Scarcity and are so good at reminding me to find the 'Art of Enough' every day. Jude, Johnty, Andy and our wonderful daughters Izzy and Iona – this book is also for you.

PERMISSIONS

NOTES AND BIBLIOGRAPHY

EPIGRAPH

1 Gore, N. (2013). Final speech from the play, 'We Will be Free' first performed in 2013. Published in 2017 in *Workers Play Time Volume 1*, Workable Books.

INTRODUCTION

1 See 'Greta Thunberg "Our House is on Fire" 2019 World Economic Forum (WEF) in Davos', 2019. Available from www.youtube.com/watch?v=zrF1THd4bUM [accessed 9 May 2021].

2 See IPCC (2018), *Special Report: Global Warming of 1.5°C*. Available from www.ipcc.ch/sr15/ [accessed 9 May 2021].

3 See Unicef, 'Every child's breath is under threat'. Available from www.unicef.org.uk/clean-air-child-health-air-pollution/ [accessed 9 May 2021].

4 Lovelock, J. (1981). *Gaia: A New Look at Life on Earth*. Oxford University Press.

5 See Solnit, R., 'The impossible has already happened': What coronavirus can teach us about hope'. *The Guardian*, 7 April 2020.

Available from www.theguardian.com/world/2020/apr/07/what-coronavirus-can-teach-us-about-hope-rebecca-solnit [accessed 9 May 2021].

ART 1: ENOUGH MINDSET

1 James, W., & Drummond, R. (1890). *The Principles of Psychology*. The exact source of this quote is unknown – it is commonly ascribed to William James, and the sentiment is reflected in the book referenced here.

2 Dweck, C. S. (2006). *Mindset: Changing the Way You Think to Fulfil Your Potential*. Random House.

3 Proust, M. (1913–1927). *In Search of Lost Time*. New edition, Penguin Books Ltd., 2002.

4 Hibberd, J. (2019). *The Imposter Cure: How to Stop Feeling Like a Fraud and Escape the Mind-Trap of Imposter Syndrome*. Aster, Octopus Publishing Group,

5 In 2010, the UK Post Office commissioned YouGov to research anxieties suffered by mobile phone users. See Elmore, T., 'Nomophobia: A rising trend in students', 18 September 2014. Available from www.psychologytoday.com/gb/blog/artificial-maturity/201409/nomophobia-rising-trend-in-students [accessed 9 May 2021].

6 Brach, T. (2000). *Radical Self-Acceptance*. Sounds True.

7 Lama, D. and Tutu, A. D. (2017). *The Book of Joy*. Ulverscroft.

8 Winnicott, D. W. (1980). *Playing and Reality*. Penguin Books.

9 Kline, N. (1998). *Time to Think: Listening to Ignite the Human Mind*. Cassell Illustrated.

10 Seligman, M. (2011). *Learned Optimism* (2nd ed.). William Heinemann.

ART 2: ENOUGH PERMISSION

1 The precise source of this quote is unknown, but it is attributed to Eleanor Roosevelt. See https://quoteinvestigator.com/2012/04/30/no-one-inferior/ [accessed 9 May 2021].

2 Obama, M. (2018). *Becoming*. Viking.

3 Obama, M. (2015). Tuskegee University commencement address, 9 May 2015. Available from https://obamawhitehouse.archives.gov/the-press-office/2015/05/09/remarks-first-lady-tuskegee-university-commencement-address [accessed 9 May 2021].

4 Santos L. Yale University Science of Happiness online course. Available from https://ggsc.berkeley.edu/what_we_do/event/the_science_of_happiness [accessed 9 May 2021].

5 Saint Augustine Quotes. (n.d.). BrainyQuote.com. Available from www.brainyquote.com/quotes/saint_augustine_107689 [accessed 4 February 2021].

6 Hendricks, G. (2010). *The Big Leap: Conquer Your Hidden Fear and Take Life to the Next Level*. HarperOne.

7 Whittington, J. (2020). *Systemic Coaching and Constellations: The Principles, Practices and Application for Individuals, Teams and Groups* (3rd ed.). Kogan Page.

8 Hellinger, B. (1998). *Love's Hidden Symmetry: What Makes Love Work in Relationships*. Zieg, Tucker & Co.

9 See 'Who are the workshop facilitators?' Available from https://constellationworkshops.co.uk/who/ [accessed 9 May 2021].

10 Chesterton, G. K. *Illustrated London News*, 14 January 1911.

11 Scharmer, C. O. (2008). *Theory U: Leading from the Future as it Emerges* (1st ed.). Meine Verlag.

12 Craig, N. (2018). *Leading from Purpose: Clarity and Confidence to Act When It Matters*. Nicholas Brealey Publishing.

13 Oliver, M. (2013). *New and Selected Poems, Volume One.* Beacon Press.

14 Pink, D. H. (2018). *Drive: The Surprising Truth About What Motivates Us.* Canongate Books.

15 Doyle, G. (2020). *Untamed: Stop Pleasing, Start Living.* Vermilion.

ART 3: ENOUGH PRESENCE

1 Cuddy, A. (2016). *Presence: Bringing Your Boldest Self to Your Biggest Challenges.* Orion.

2 Csikszentmihalyi, M. (2008). *Flow: The Psychology of Optimal Experience.* HarperPerennial.

3 Levine, P. A. (2010). *In an Unspoken Voice: How the Body Releases Trauma and Restores Goodness.* North Atlantic Books.

4 See www.heartmath.org

5 Childre, D. and Rozman, D. (2005). *Transforming Stress: The HeartMath Solution for Relieving Worry, Fatigue and Tension.* New Harbinger Publications.

6 Goleman, D. (1996). *Emotional Intelligence: Why It Can Matter More Than IQ.* Bloomsbury Publishing PLC.

7 Rock, D. (2009). *Your Brain at Work: Strategies for Overcoming Distraction, Regaining Focus, and Working Smarter All Day Long.* HarperCollins.

8 Rodenburg, P. (2008). *The Second Circle: Using Positive Energy for Success in Every Situation.* W. W. Norton & Company.

9 Watts, A. (1951). *The Wisdom of Insecurity.* Vintage Books.

10 Tolle, E. (2005). *The Power of Now: A Guide to Spiritual Enlightenment.* Hodder Paperback.

11 Hebb, D. (1949). *The Organization of Behavior: A Neuropsychological Theory*. Wiley.

12 Woollett, K. and Maguire, E. A. (2011). Acquiring 'the Knowledge' of London's layout drives structural brain changes. *Current Biology*. See https://wellcome.ac.uk/press-release/changes-london-taxi-drivers-brains-driven-acquiring-'-knowledge-study-shows [accessed 9 May 2021].

13 Seligman, M. (2011). *Learned Optimism* (2nd ed.). North Sydney: William Heinemann.

14 Nerburn, K. (1998). *Small Graces: The Quiet Gifts of Everyday Life*. New World Library.

ART 4: ENOUGH BOUNDARIES

1 Davies, W. H. 'Leisure', published in Davies, W. H. (2011). *Songs of Joy and Others*. A. C. Fifield.

2 Senge, P. M. (1999). *The Fifth Discipline: The Art & Practice of the Learning Organization*. Image Books.

3 Wheatley, M. J. (2006). *Leadership and the New Science*. Berrett-Koehler.

4 Bailey, P. C. (2017). *The Productivity Project: Accomplishing More by Managing Your Time, Attention, and Energy*. Crown Business.

5 Newport, C. (2016). *Deep Work: Rules for Focused Success in a Distracted World*. Piatkus Books.

6 Webb, C. (2017). *How to Have a Good Day: The Essential Toolkit for a Productive Day at Work and Beyond*. Pan Books.

7 Elizabeth Gilbert talks about this on her Instagram feed.

8 Kline, N. (1998). *Time to Think: Listening to Ignite the Human Mind*. Cassell Illustrated.

9 See Stone, L. 'Beyond simple multi-tasking: Continuous partial attention'. Available from https://lindastone.net/2009/11/30/beyond-simple-multi-tasking-continuous-partial-attention/ [accessed 9 May 2021].

10 Collins, J. (2006). *Good to Great*. Random House Business Books.

11 Brown, B. (2018). *Dare to Lead: Brave Work. Tough Conversations. Whole Hearts*. Random House.

12 Quoted in Webb, C. (2017). *How to Have a Good Day: The Essential Toolkit for a Productive Day at Work and Beyond*. Pan Books.

ART 5: ENOUGH RESOURCE

1 Behn, A. (1984). *The Lucky Chance*. Methuen Publishing.

2 Songwriters: Gerald Marks / Seymour Simons, All of Me lyrics © Sony/ATV Music Publishing LLC, Round Hill Music Big Loud Songs, Songtrust Ave, Warner Chappell Music, Inc, Kobalt Music Publishing Ltd., Marlong Music Corp.

3 Whyte, D. (2002). *Crossing the Unknown Sea: Work and the Shaping of Identity*. Penguin Books.

4 See www.alanwatts.com

5 Hellinger, B. (1998). *Love's Hidden Symmetry: What Makes Love Work in Relationships*. Zieg, Tucker & Co.

6 Mate, G. (2013). *In the Realm of Hungry Ghosts: Close Encounters with Addiction*. Random House.

7 Sandberg, S. and Grant, A. (2017). *Option B: Facing Adversity, Building Resilience, and Finding Joy*. W H Allen.

8 Kolb, D. (1984). *Experiential Learning: Experience as the Source of Learning and Development*. Prentice-Hall.

9 Tedeschi, R. and Calhoun, L. (2003). *Helping Bereaved Parents: A Clinician's Guide*. Routledge.

10 Wageman, R., Nunes, D. A., Burruss, J. A. and Hackman, J. R. (2008). *Senior Leadership Teams: What It Takes to Make Them Great*. Harvard Business Review Press.

11 Kouzes, J. M. and Posner, B. Z. (2017). *The Leadership Challenge: How to Make Extraordinary Things Happen in Organizations* (6th ed.). John Wiley & Sons.

12 Lencioni, P. M. (2002). *The Five Dysfunctions of a Team: A Leadership Fable* (1st ed.). Jossey-Bass.

13 Lamott, A. (1994). *Bird by Bird: Some Instructions on Writing and Life*. Pantheon Books.

14 Brailsford is quoted in Syed, M. (2015). *Black Box Thinking: Why Most People Never Learn from Their Mistakes—But Some Do*. John Murray.

15 Clear, J. (2018). *Atomic Habits: An Easy and Proven Way to Build Good Habits and Break Bad Ones*. Random House Business Books.

ART 6: ENOUGH GROWTH

1 Smart, U., from 'Poor Man's Lamentation', public domain. The Full English online archive. Found and set to music by Hannah James in 'Songs of Separation'.

2 Carle, E. (1969). *The Very Hungry Caterpillar*. The World Publishing Company.

3 Handy, C. (2016). *The Second Curve: Thoughts on Reinventing Society*. Random House Business Books.

4 Fitzgerald, F. S. (1925). *The Great Gatsby*. Penguin Classics.

5 Mate, G. (2013). *In the Realm of Hungry Ghosts: Close Encounters with Addiction*. Random House.

6 Schumacher, E. F. (1973). *Small is Beautiful: A Study of Economics as if People Mattered*. Frederick Muller.

7 Raworth, K. (2018). *Doughnut Economics: Seven Ways to Think Like a 21st-century Economist*. Random House Business Books.

8 Meadows, D. H., Randers, J. and Meadows, D. L. (2004). *The Limits to Growth: The 30-year Update*. Earthscan.

9 See 'Dana (Donella) Meadows lecture: Sustainable systems', 8 May 2013. Available from www.youtube.com/watch?v=HMmChiLZZHg [accessed 9 May 2021].

10 Leonard, A. (2010). *The Story of Stuff: How Our Obsession with Stuff Is Trashing the Planet, Our Communities, and Our Health – and a Vision for Change*. Constable. www.storyofstuff.org

11 Jackson, T. (2010). *An Economic Reality Check*. TED Talk. Available from www.ted.com/talks/tim_jackson_an_economic_reality_check?language=en [accessed 9 May 2021].

12 Gandhi quote cited in *Small is Beautiful* by E. F. Schumacher.

13 Robert Kennedy, speech transcript, University of Kansas, 18 March 1968. Available from www.jfklibrary.org/learn/about-jfk/the-kennedy-family/robert-f-kennedy/robert-f-kennedy-speeches/remarks-at-the-university-of-kansas-march-18-1968 [accessed 9 May 2021].

14 For the doughnut infographic, see https://commons.wikimedia.org/wiki/File:Doughnut_(economic_model).jpg [accessed 9 May 2021].

15 Raworth, K. (2018). *Doughnut Economics: Seven Ways to Think like a 21st-century Economist*. Random House Business Books.

16 Grahame, K. (1908). *The Wind in the Willows*. Vintage Children's Classics.

17 Rock, D. (2009). *Your Brain at Work: Strategies for Overcoming Distraction, Regaining Focus, and Working Smarter All Day Long.* HarperCollins.

18 Kondo, M. (2017). *Spark Joy: An Illustrated Guide to the Japanese Art of Tidying.* Vermilion.

19 Leunig, M. 'Joy of Missing Out'. Available from www.leunig. com.au/works/recent-cartoons/769-jomo [accessed 9 May 2021].

20 *David Attenborough: A Life on Our Planet.* Available from www.netflix.com/gb/title/80216393 [accessed 9 May 2021].

21 Ellen MacArthur Foundation, *Towards the Circular Economy.* Available from www.ellenmacarthurfoundation.org/circular-economy/concept/infographic [accessed 9 May 2021].

22 Bentham, J. (1789). *An Introduction to the Principles of Morals and Legislation*, 1996 edition, edited by J. H. Burns and H. L. A. Hart. Clarendon Press.

23 Eisenstein, C. (2018). *Climate: A New Story.* North Atlantic Books.

24 Rozenthuler, S. (2020). *Powered by Purpose.* Pearson Education.

ART 7: ENOUGH CONNECTION

1 Shakespeare, W., *Troilus and Cressida*, Act III, Scene III.

2 Brown, B. (2012). *Daring Greatly: How the Courage to be Vulnerable Transforms the Way We Live, Love, Parent and Lead.* Hay House UK.

3 World Economic Forum, 'How has the world's urban population changed from 1950 to today?'. Available from www.weforum. org/agenda/2020/11/global-continent-urban-population-urbanisation-percent/ [accessed 9 May 2021].

4 Forster, E.M. (1910). *Howards End*. Penguin Classics.

5 Brown, B. (2015). *Rising Strong*. Vermilion.

6 Kahane, A. (2010). *Power and Love: A Theory and Practice of Social Change* (1st ed.). Berrett-Koehler.

7 hooks, b. (2001). *All About Love: New Visions*. William Morrow & Company.

8 See 'Our vision, mission and values'. Available from www.jocoxfoundation.org/vision [accessed 9 May 2021].

9 Dilts, R., Hallbom, T. and Smith, S. (2012). *Beliefs: Pathways to Health and Well-Being* (2nd ed.). Crown House Publishing.

10 Raworth, K. (2018). *Doughnut Economics: Seven Ways to Think Like a 21st-century Economist*. Random House Business Books.

11 Norberg-Hodge, H. (2019). *Local is our Future: Steps to an Economics of Happiness*. Local Futures.

12 Krznaric, R. (2020). *The Good Ancestor: How to Think Long Term in a Short-Term World*. Penguin, Random House.

13 Quoted in *The Good Ancestor* (cited above).

14 Frankl, V. E. (1959). *Man's Search for Meaning*. Ebury Publishing.

15 See 'Fall 2005 commencement address by Chief Oren Lyons', 22 May 2005. Available from https://nature.berkeley.edu/news/2005/05/fall-2005-commencement-address-chief-oren-lyons [accessed 9 May 2021].

16 Eisenstein, C. (2011). *Sacred Economics: Money, Gift, and Society in the Age of Transition*. North Atlantic Books.

17 See 'The Great Green Wall'. Available from www.greatgreenwall.org/about-great-green-wall [accessed 9 May 2021].

18 See https://treesisters.org

19 Benyus, J. 'Biomimicry', 11 September 2015. Available from youtube.com/watch?v=sf4oW8OtaPY&t=778s [accessed 9 May 2021].

20 Norberg-Hodge, H. (2019). *Local is our Future: Steps to an Economics of Happiness*. Local Futures.